Alan Lowndes

by

Jonathan Riley

Cover: 'Coronation Street, Stockport', 28 x 36 inches, Oil on Board, 1961 (Private Collection)
Inner Cover Front and Back: Scarf designed by Alan Lowndes when working for Julius Frank, late 1940s - *see Chapter 3 for details* (Private collection of Rosemary Howarth, Alan Lowndes's niece)

Detail of 'Three Musical Clowns', *32 x 28 inches, Oil on Board, 1960 (Collection of the Artist)*

For Alan and Valerie

Down as you like in the circling dusk
With Valerie and Alan Lowndes
This room is like an exploded bomb
Is battered by those extra sounds.

The fiddle sounds as Alan plays
An empty bottle or a tray.
Or by the brain of Stockport
Each object loses its own way.

I have seen the grisly bear
Taken by a maiden's hand.
I have seen the Stockport boys
Passing in the Stockport band.

I have had my fill of free
Days and talked in the betting yard.
I mean my friend, Alan Lowndes,
Walking up to stamp his card.

O, Alan, sing The Jasper Sea
Or sing about the Old Grey Duck.
A painter is a painter if
Upon his medium he can cluck.

'Implies a sense of humour' says
The catalogue I have.
A sense of humour is a sense
Of the incongruousness of love.

Then, Alan, may you love your while
As love could live on Wharf Street.
You are shaped by Stockport
Although your hopes have shaped your feet.

So now in the Cornish dusk
With Valerie become your spouse
I am a happy poetry boy
To have you loose about my house.

And now the lines are ending
For every creature has its fill.
The lover must lie down to love.
The Artist must go over the hill.

W. S. Graham

Grateful Thanks

The author would like to thank many people for their very kind assistance with the production of this book, but especially Valerie, Rosalind and Mandy Lowndes for their help, patience and forbearance. Ron Thomas, Jack Harris, Ray Boston, Slim Ingram and Marion Demount were kind enough to meet and write to the author on many occasions. Grateful thanks to many other people too numerous to mention, but whose aid and advice has been invaluable; sadly a number of very kind and helpful people are no longer with us. The author would particularly like to thank Frances Christie, Geoff Hassell, Jan White, Pat Williams and Sarah Flynn for their most valuable advice and comments. Grateful thanks to Michael and Margaret Snow for their kind permission to reproduce poems and letters by Sydney Graham, and also to Leon Suddaby for permission to quote from the writings of Alan Lowndes. Many thanks to Nigel Beechy for his technical assistance without which the book would be impossible and to Simon Rufus for his technical assisitance. Grateful thanks to the support from Andras Kalman and Robin Light at the Crane Kalman Gallery, 178 Brompton Road, London and to Sir Michael Parkinson for kindly writing the Forward. Finally the book would not have been possible without the endless patience and energy of the author's wife, Alison, who drove him many miles to interview people all round the country and to read through the drafts of the book - tibi multas gratias ago.

Footnotes

All quotations from Alan Lowndes have been taken from his brief autobiography entitled 'Confessions of a Provincial Bohemian', started in 1977 but never completed, and also two unpublished essays entitled 'Why We Paint' (1978) and 'The Day I Died' (1978), as well as extensive correspondece with Andras Kalman and Elizabeth Boston. All other footnotes are extracts from conversations or correspondence with the author between 2003 and 2009, unless otherwise stated. The originator of any quotation has been given in the footnotes, except for statements by Alan Lowndes. All written quotations throughout the book have been reproduced exactly as they were written without any correction of grammar, spelling or motive.

Ownership of Paintings

Wherever possible the ownership of paintings is stated, unless the whereabouts of a painting is unknown. The ownership of the paintings has been given at the time the author received an image of the painting. Several have changed hands since then, some several times.

Images of Paintings

The author would like to thank the following for their very kind assistance with digital images for the book: Freya Mitton and her staff at Sothebys; Emma Corke and Matthew Bradbury and their staff at Bonhams; William Porter and his staff at Christies; Capes Dunn Auction House, Manchester; Lord Harris of Peckham; Andy Firth at the Stockport Museum and Art Gallery; William Gibbs; Bill Clark, Clark Fine Art; Michael Bowman, Michael Bowman Auctions; Morrigan Ellis at the Clwyd Fine Arts Trust; James Huntington-Whitely; Michael Sweeney; Tennants Auctioneers, Leyburn; Manya Igel of Manya Igel Fine Art; Betty Goldfield; Diane Lovelock; Kristian Day of David Messum Fine Art Limited and all the many people who most generously allowed the author into their homes to photograph their paintings.

Dimensions of Images

All dimensions of images are shown in inches, height by width. Alan often confused the recording of dimensions by writing them as width by height in his Catalogue Raisonné: his method was copied in early catalogues.

First Published in 2010 by Construction Arts Ltd

© Jonathan Riley

ISBN 978-0-9560505-1-9

All rights reserved. No part of this publication may be reproduced, stored in a retrieval system, or transmitted in any form or by any means, electronic, mechanical or otherwise without prior permission of the author.

Printed by Nordic Group, Five Acres, Stone Street, Stanford South, Ashford, Kent, TN25 6DE. Tel: 01303 813722, Fax: 01303 812115; Email: sales@nordicservices.co.uk; Web: www.nordicservices.co.uk

Alan Lowndes, born 1921, died 1978

Contents

Chapter 1 -   Heaton Norris, Cheshire - the early days

Chapter 2 -   World War II

Chapter 3 -   Tom, Ron, Frieda - the late Forties and early Fifties

Chapter 4 -   Elizabeth Horsfield and Andras Kalman (1919 -2007)

Chapter 5 -   St. Ives

Chapter 6 -   Stockport, Portraits, The Circus, Lowry

Chapter 7 -   John and Anne Willett, Vence, Valerie, Marriage and Honeymoon in Normandy

Chapter 8 -   Cornwall Part 1, 1959 to the mid Sixties, Life in St. Ives and Halestown

Chapter 9 -   Cornwall Part 2 - Aspects of Life, Art and Drinking in Cornwall until 1970

Chapter 10 - Gloucestershire 1970 to 1975

Chapter 11 - Catastrophe, Illness, Happiness and Finale

Forward by Sir Michael Parkinson

"I have been aware of Alan Lowndes in the best of situations. There was a very good pub near Granada Television in the early sixties run by an eccentric landlord called Arthur Gosling. Mr Gosling not only pulled a great pint but also had an eye for a painting. He had in his pub ten, maybe fifteen, canvases by Lowndes - some of them, it was rumoured, had been donated by the artist when he was unable to pay his bar bill. These paintings created a wonderful, colourful and fascinating backdrop to an evening's drinking. Then I met one of Alan's biggest and most influential enthusiasts Andras Kalman. It was Andras who persuaded me to start to collect his work - not that I needed much persuasion. Over the years I have owned maybe eight or nine of his paintings and have found great enjoyment in the artist's work whether it be in the streets of Stockport or the leafy lanes of Devon. I met him on three or four occasions and found him an easy man to get along with. I think he is a significant painter of a Northern landscape long gone and, as with all the best painters, his work is as much a social comment on a lost culture as well as a picture of a bygone age."

Chapter 1 - Heaton Norris - the early days

'I have found a Modigliani of the streets.' - Charles Laughton
'Alan Lowndes is a greater painter than Lowry.' - Sir Terry Frost

Alan Lowndes entered the world on a cold and wet February day in 1921. He joined his siblings Sam (Junior), Jenny and Colin in their terraced house in Heaton Norris in the upper part of the Cheshire mill town of Stockport. Unfortunately, his older brother Stanley had died in infancy. By all accounts his mother Jenny was a beautiful woman, and most of her children inherited her delicate beauty: certainly Alan was fortunate to do so. Sam, his father, worked for the L.M.S. Railway Company as a clerk, a respected steady job in those days. Jenny (nee Murray) came from Kilmarnock, where her father worked as a blacksmith. The name Lowndes can mean 'dear or beloved' from the Old English Leofun, or 'bear cub' from 'hun'. Both definitions were to be amazingly apt for Alan's personality and character as he progressed through life.

SAM AND JENNY LOWNDES'S MARRIAGE CERTIFICATE, AUGUST 15TH 1908

'SAM LOWNDES SENIOR AT CHRISTINE'S WEDDING'. Christine was Alan's younger sister; she married Eric and had three children, Susan, Rosemary and Philip. Throughout the book Sam Lowndes, Alan's father, is referred to as Sam Senior to avoid any muddle with Sam, his oldest son, who is desribed as Sam Junior. Just to complicate matters, grandfather was also named Sam.

LEFT PAGE:

'SELF PORTRAIT, TO CILLI'.

25 x 18.5 inches, Oil on Card, 1953 (Collection of the Artist)

It is very difficult to imagine the family home in Oxford Street, so much has been pulled down or 'improved'. Life revolved around the kitchen, especially the table. There was no bathroom, only a sink and a water tap. Three houses in a rear yard known as 'the big yard' shared the outside lavatory. As Alan said later, "None of this worried us, we didn't even know it was a slum, slums were always somewhere else. The term 'deprived' wasn't even invented then." When he was a little older, he and some friends decided to cycle to 'find some slums': he had no concept he lived in one. Many of the Lowndes's neighbours were Irish: McGuiness, Hennessey, O'Malley or Connolly. Interestingly, Alan's older daughter, Mandy, used to play the fiddle in an Irish band in Manchester each Thursday evening.

Sadly his mother Jenny died when he was three. "I can hardly remember my mother. I only have one memory of her. She was in the kitchen looking lovely and in tears. On the piano in the front room my dad was playing 'Ye banks and braes O'Bonnie Doon'. Her soft looking auburn hair I remember vividly. I was three years old and I faintly remember being dressed in black new clothes, but that's about all I remember."

Alan suffered from a severe stammer. There have been several stories alleging the cause of this affliction. Across the road from the Lowndes's house was a cattle pen, where the cows and sheep were kept before being killed in the slaughterhouse of a butcher's shop on the corner of the street. Marion Demount, who also lived in the same street, relates that a cow escaped from its pen and chased Alan's mother. Alan saw the whole episode, which so alarmed the young boy that a stammer developed. In his own account, he had nightmares and woke screaming because of the bellows of the cattle. For one reason or another he was nervous of cows and bulls for the rest of his life. 'To see them being driven through the streets with their wild desperate eyes would frighten me.' Later he would crowd into the bedroom window of his friend Fred's house to watch the slaughterhouse killing across the street.

Sam Lowndes was left a widower in a small terraced house with a full time job and five children. In the early days Granny Murray was responsible for much of the care of the children, while Sam was at work. She was assisted by Auntie Nellie, who regarded Alan as her favourite. Later his sister Jenny was to take up much of the burden. Jenny was a strong character. "She was the boss of both her husbands: both were very nice decent men."[1] Sam's single parent situation was not so unusual at that time, many families had suffered deaths in the Great War, though normally it was the mother who was left to bring up the children. Nevertheless, it must have been quite a problem for Sam to cope with his life and extensive family.

OXFORD STREET, HEATON NORRIS 2003, *The part of the street where the Lowndes lived has been demolished.*

1 Slim Ingram. Slim was a theatre impresario who married Sam Junior's daughter, Jill.

Top: Sam Lowndes Junior

Lower left: Jenny Lowndes

Lower Right: Colin Lowndes

Sam (father) was in his own way quite a remarkable man. His father, also named Sam, lived near Wilmslow in Lacey Green in a cottage with a garden and trees at the back. Grandfather Sam too was quite a character: he had married a schoolteacher - 'a real D.H. Lawrence situation' as Alan put it. He had seven sons of whom sadly only two survived, Uncle George and Sam. Alan never met Uncle George, although Alan hinted that Uncle George had risen in the world to become a teacher in a Public School. Grandfather Sam had a considerable reputation: amongst many tales, he was alleged to be able to lift a barrel of beer with his teeth. By the time Alan met his grandfather, he regarded him as a simmered down character and recalled him being fondly dignified towards his grandchildren.

Alan's father, Sam, was a sparky small man, verbally astute and "prone to lob grenades into conversations to see what happened".[2] "Sam was a somewhat dandified Steptoe character. He was very outgoing and always turned every conversation round to his ideas and was

2 Peter Lowndes, the son of Colin Lowndes

'LANCASHIRE STREET'. *14 x 18 inches, Oil on Canvas, 1951 (Private Collection)*

very tight with his money. Sam would read books, and that would become knowledge to him, he then made these statements."[3] There is no doubt that Alan inherited his father's conversational style. Sam was also very musical. Whenever there was a visiting singer at the local theatre, Sam was usually summoned to be the accompanist on the piano, especially for G.H. Elliott, 'the Chocolate Coloured Coon'. "My dad was a real living it up man, he was a stifled creative person." He was a real 'nutcase' according to Mae, Sam Junior's wife; he allowed all his children to do as they pleased.

There is no doubt that he was a very intelligent man, who did much to stimulate conversation in his household. He was also sensitive to the creative arts, as well as being a keen musician. Sam must have been quite unusual for a parent in the traditional working class environment around him and considered himself as such. "He had this attitude, that all his family inherited, that they were a step above everyone else. They didn't speak to neighbours."[3] Sam played a huge role in Alan's development.

Sam worked 'turns', as they were called in those days. He was fortunate to enjoy his 'railway' perk of free travel passes for his family. As Alan described it, "We became railway children during his holidays. We travelled everywhere for the day. We could get there, but we couldn't afford to stay, not even for one night. I think we covered most of the L.M.S. network. On this basis I went to London aged about 6 or 7 ... The big free shows in London were the Art Galleries. The National and the Tate were always visited. One time we visited the Royal Academy, where Stanley Spencer was the main exhibitor at the time. I had vivid 'Spencerian' dreams for some time afterwards. Other low priced places we visited were the Zoo and the Tower of London. I think people don't realise how much children record and absorb in their early lives." Alan always appreciated what Sam had achieved for his family and the enriching experiences these trips provided. He lamented later with his own family that he could not persuade the children of friends to join him on such outings.

Alan was rather pleased in a way that his father was a very impractical man with his hands. "We were spared the agonies of the cat's whisker as radio was beginning: the first radio our family saw at home was a sleek Ferranti." The wireless remained a source of pleasure all his life. There was a strong bond in the family. All the children were bright and had a 'presence'. Maybe their upbringing was remarkably stimulating considering all the difficulties Sam faced.

School beckoned; in 1926 aged five Alan joined Christ Church C.E. School just round the corner. He did not last long his first day and slipped back home, only to be brought back by Granny Murray. Christ Church was divided into Infants, Junior and Senior. Alan was happy enough in the Infants section, where his stammer did not really matter. He claimed he had several fights with the boys, but liked all the girls. Names such as Doris, Joan, Hannah, Mabel, Marion or Mary appealed to him. He particularly recalled sitting near a girl called Doris and would gaze at her dark brown eyes, hair and plump little arms. He executed his first ever drawing of Joyce, who played Cupid in the school pantomime. She wore a short white tunic, knickers and tinsel wings. Sadly the friendship never ripened.

From the Infants section he moved to the Juniors and began his 'man' training. His stammer became an agony. "Red faced virago women teachers screamed at me to 'Spit it out', or laughed, which was worse. Outside school I was no longer a toddler. In shops I was treated as an idiot, giggled and laughed at. To make it worse I was very sensitive and emotional, but I was growing less frightened of people. They all thought my stammer was a sign of cowardice. This attitude remained well into my time in the army. As a result, I got into fights quite often, and I'm not really a fighting man. Being born in the North, being small and slight of build was a handicap enough, the stammer made it worse." On the positive side, he learned to use his stammer to buy some time while observing people around him. Many have attested to the effective use of his stammer in later life. Alan's early school experiences were to mark him for life, especially without a mother to comfort him. He used to say that he wanted a mother, but could not bear being 'mothered'. He claimed that he loved women, but they tortured him, because they knew he could never love one particular one. This somewhat egotistical statement is not borne out by the facts, especially

3 Slim Ingram

his one sided relationship with Elizabeth Horsfield in the Fifties.

School was his biggest misery, but he was extremely bright and could master the required work with ease. Nevertheless, reading out loud to the class was purgatory. Like so many boys in his position, he became lazy and somewhat troublesome and earned his fair ration of canings. He never begrudged his teachers; it was very difficult to cope with 50 in the class. He showed little aptitude for art at this stage, finding it difficult to keep his paper free of smudges and marks when drawing his cubes, cones and cylinders, but he came into his own when pupils were allowed to draw freehand.

He was a very small boy for his age with lovely wavy dark hair. He was able to use these assets to conduct early relationships with some of the girls, alas without any success. He found that the girls tended to admire the sporty types; he was no good at sport and could not compete, especially with his stammer. One or two of the girls deigned to play with him, mostly at mothers and fathers. The games always ended with their hands between their legs exploring knickers and pants. He did not place girls on a pedestal, only boys without sisters did that.

He was slowly developing his interest in drawing at home on the all important kitchen table. Sam used to draw for his children, 'as dads do'. Alan, brother Colin and his friend Fred drew battle scenes - Normans and Saxons, Germans and British with great gusto; Fred and Colin soon lost interest. Alan did not. He mostly copied comic cartoon figures like Mickey Mouse and other Disney characters.

THE SENIOR CLASS, CHRIST CHURCH SCHOOL, HEATON NORRIS, STOCKPORT. *Alan is not featured in this photo, he was too young.*

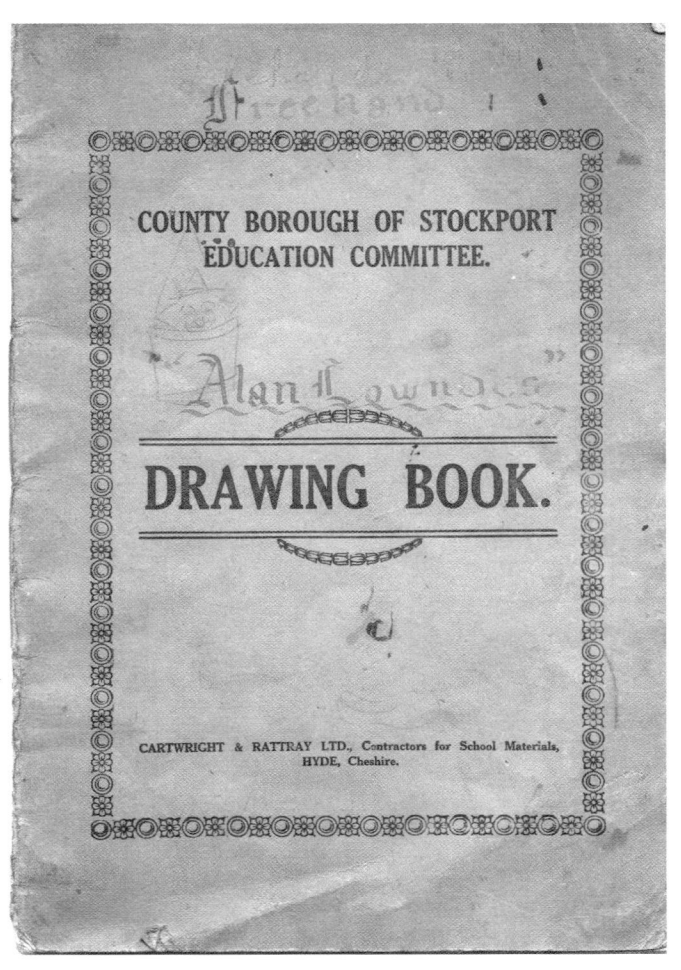

Alan's drawing book, aged 11

'The Final Plunge'

'Don Julio' 'Dame Clara Cluck'

The nearest chip shop was one of his delights. "Tatty but clean inside it had a refinement of wrapping the chips first in blank white paper and then newspaper. Armed with a Black Prince pencil, I would volunteer to fetch the chips any time. I used to pinch a few of the smaller sheets, which they cut for wrapping the fish each time I went. Sometimes I couldn't wait to get home and did little drawings, Mickey Mouse usually on the corners of the big white sheets. I used to draw about three sheets down from the top, so that when my turn came, they would flip down unnoticed. I first realised I wanted to be an artist at this stage. I wanted more people to see my drawings. Showing off - art is a lot of showing off."

Alan left school at 14 years of age. He took an active part in the Scouts at the insistence of his brothers, which helped overcome his 'anti organisation attitudes'. Sam ran the Wolf Pack as cub master, and Colin was a leading member. Alan enjoyed the camps in the grounds of a big house near Prestbury with the bell tents and lovely Cheshire scenery. He gained a few badges in the Scouts, the Artist's Badge of course and became the first ever member of his group to become a King's Scout. His other first in the family was a badge for swimming 25 yards in the 'fateful' Stockport Baths (see the next chapter for details).

Sam Junior was the oldest sibling. Slim Ingram, his son in law feels that the Scouts were a way for Sam to gain self-respect. He was a car mechanic and was not very talented in other ways. Sadly Sam and his wife, Mae lost their son John aged 19 in a car accident. John borrowed a car and drove too fast round a bend in Rhyl and killed himself and two nurses in the crash. Mae, a talented seamstress, was employed by Slim to make costumes for his theatre. On one occasion, the actress Mia Farrow asked Mae to come with her to America to look after her child. Unfortunately Farrow divorced her husband so there was no job. Mae's sister Dora was a very intelligent woman and trained as a chemist. She ran the chemist's shop in Stockport, which in those days was more like a doctor's surgery. "It was the old fashioned shop where you went along and said 'I don't feel so well, can you mix me a bottle of something to make me better?' Sadly in the end, as society changed the only thing that kept her shop going was the sale of condoms."[4]

After leaving school, Alan had to make a choice about earning a living. "I could not decide what the hell I wanted to do." His brother Sam's friend ran a painting and decorating business. Alan joined him as an apprentice in 1935 aged fourteen, and "he and I were the

4 Slim Ingram

RIGHT PAGE:
'THE CHIP SHOP',
30 x 20 inches, Oil on Canvas, 1970

business." All the while he was reading as much as he could and seeing as many paintings as possible, "which wasn't a lot and not very good at that". Alan continued his association with the scouts. He could never fathom why all his activity as a decorator's apprentice and hiking and camping at the week-end didn't alter his muscle development. As he said, "I felt like the joke about the Charles Atlas course. Dear Sir, I have done all the things you said, can you please send the muscles."

As an apprentice, Alan attended night classes in the decorator's class at the 'tech', now Stockport College of Science and Technology, which compensated for his lowly position in his day-to-day work. The drawing sessions were rigidly concentrated on the ornament of classical sculpture and heraldry. Other sessions were composed of lettering, graining and marbling and the composition of paint. As an apprentice he used the old method of mixing linseed oil with primers, undercoats and ground coats for many arm aching hours. This arduous activity left him with a lasting invaluable knowledge of oil paint. "Should the paint factory system collapse, I could carry on." He was interested in the graining course, it gave him an insight into wood grain, whereas marbling only showed him the tools used, no marble being available.

At work, he found the actual decorating of houses rather tiresome: it was smelly, damp, colic and arduous. Often he was working outside in the biting cold or in empty dirty houses. Sometimes he had to cycle for miles before starting work at 8 a.m., or he had to push a handcart loaded with ladders, buckets, paint etc. for long distances, often in very bad weather. Both riding and pushing were made even more arduous and uncomfortable by the cobbled streets.

LEFT PAGE (16): DETAIL OF 'AUNT DORA'S SHOP', *(Stockport), 14 x 10 inches, Oil on Canvas, 1967, (Collection of Slim Ingram)*

'THE BARROW', *32 x 25.5 inches, Oil on Board, 1958 (Collection of the Crane Kalman Gallery)*

ABOVE: WILLIAM TURNER (B.1920), 'THE CART' *Alan used to meet the painter, William Turner, occasionally in a coffee bar in Manchester to discuss art. Turner's work has become much sought after in recent times.*

Whilst hanging their 'nauseous wallpaper' he used the opportunity to carry out large drawings on the 'lovely white plaster underneath'. He felt uncomfortable and negative in the large houses of the middle classes, developing quite a feeling for the politics of envy. He was particularly upset by the 'posh voice', as are many Northeners, and continued to be so for the rest of his life. Some years later, Sam Senior, his father, once offered to pay his bus fare to Alderley Edge, home to some of Manchester's wealthiest and most sophisticated commuters, for him to paint more commercially viable views than the slums of Stockport. All to no avail, he painted what he wanted to and that was that. Take it or leave it, he was certainly not going to massage middle class egos.

Chapter 2 - World War II

In the summer of 1939 the Boy Scouts went on a camping holiday to the Isle of Man. Catching the ferry and sailing across to the island must have been quite an adventure for a young man whose travel had been entirely limited to the railway network. By then Alan was a Rover Scout of long standing. The weather was absolutely glorious, and the youngsters imagined themselves to be in the Mediterranean. By the end of the camp, talk of war was everywhere, especially in the papers and on the radio. Alan recalled that shame was the emotion in the cinemas, when Chamberlain was showing his 'white paper', which claimed Hitler had peaceful intentions. The cinema audience looked with amazement and contempt at the rejoicing crowds in London. "Dead silence in the cinema was the North's reaction. In 1939 a grim relief spread about."

By chance Colin, Fred and Alan were attending the swimming baths in Stockport early one summer's evening. Unfortunately the baths were shut for a gala, the only pool open to them was very small and was known contemptuously as the Dolly Tub. While they were mooning about, Colin said to Alan, "You ought to join the army, kid". Fred backed him up. The recruiting sergeant was mildly surprised to see such an unlikely person offering his services. The idea was that Colin and Alan would be in the same unit; the date was August 28th, 1939. Alan successfully completed his medical weighing 112 lbs, with a 34 inch waist and a height of 5 feet 3 inches. Alan hadn't needed much persuasion, he hated his decorating job, and like many young men, war offered an opportunity to leave his daily drudgery and life at home. "I left my trade with as little regret as I left my school." Men have short memories; it was only twenty-one years earlier that 'the war to end all wars' had ended with a scale of slaughter unprecedented in history. Such is the boredom and quest for adventure in the young.

Left to Right:

Eric,
Christine Lowndes,
Colin Lowndes and
a friend, 1949. *Later, Eric and Christine married.*

At first Alan joined the Territorials, his brother Colin had been a 'Terrier' since 1938, but was very soon called up to the Cheshire Regiment as a private. He had made the first major decision of his life, or rather it was made for him. Sam Junior was the oldest brother, but Alan saw little of him. Colin was his older brother and traditionally led for Alan to follow. From Christmas 1939 he never saw Colin again for the duration of the war. On 29th of May, 1942 the Cheshires set sail for the Middle East via Africa to avoid the terrible threat of German U boats. They rounded the Cape and sailed up the east coast to their destination, Cairo, taking two months to arrive. Alan took part in the desert war leading up to El Alamein as a member of a Vickers gun crew.

Not much is known about his military service, as he said, "a private learned to keep his head down." He had inherited some of his father's musical talent and was one of the Regiment's buglers for Reveille. His friend, Ron Thomas, tells an amusing tale of Alan's military exploits. "I met a man at a studio I was working at, M.A. Orton. This man was in the medical corps in North Africa and he said, 'Either German or Italian planes came in low from our right and everyone dived for cover. They screamed overhead terrifying us, as we lay as low as we could. One small man stood up in the back of a truck with a Bren gun and went rat tat tat shooting without stopping. The planes went over us and headed for the hill to the side of us with the gun still firing away.' Unfortunately on the hilltop was company H.Q.. Alan of course continued firing spraying his own H.Q. with a hail of bullets.

That was typical of Alan, he wouldn't take his finger off the trigger." There must have been a mighty row afterwards. No one can remember when Alan did this, presumably it was in 1942 or early 1943 before the invasion of Sicily.

He was transferred to the photo reconnaissance unit, where he could use his drawing skills to interpret photographs. He found the new Company much more congenial than his days as a private in a regiment of the line. He claimed he had been prone to a number of diseases whilst in the desert, especially amoebic dysentery, which was to affect his liver and to leave it permanently damaged, though it is interesting to note that he passed as Grade A medically fit on his release. Alan certainly developed a very strong taste for cigarettes and alcohol during his service in the army.

The Cheshire Regiment played a distinguished part in the allied advance from Africa to Italy, and Alan came with them as part of his new unit.

ALAN'S WAR RECORD:

He was awarded the Africa Star and the Italy Star.

Alan was given a surprisingly favourable and foresighted reference by the army.

Despite the 88mm gun being ever present, he enjoyed his time in Italy, whether he was practising his soldier's Italian by 'women chasing', boozing or viewing wonderful paintings. One evening he wanted to visit the cinema, but his Italian was not so fluent muddling camera with cinema. The young lady misinterpreted what he said and ended up in his bedroom. He was not complaining, 'one can go to the cinema anytime'. "I was lucky in one way that I saw a lot of things by people who I didn't know, like Giotto. I later revisited these and found them just as fascinating with 'all the gloss' of history on them. Fra Angelico, Benozzo Gozzoli, Michelangelo hit me like a brick. I had a leave earlier in Rome, but Florence was the place I really revelled in. Venice, where I spent one day, was incredible to me in the full sense of the word."

He was particularly interested in the frescoes, especially by Fra Angelico. His early contacts with the building trade taught him about plastering, floating, skimming and plasterers themselves, whom he described as a moody lot. He could see where bits had been chipped out and done again. "This taught me that it's results that count in art, but there is generally a set pattern to arrive at these results ... No one gets a prize for getting it right the first time, but you have got to get it right. As Lowry once told me, 'Do it as good as you can, then leave it'." He was fortunate at the end of the war to attend an art class in Florence as part of the repatriation scheme preparing soldiers for civilian life.

Towards the end of the war, Alan sent home some drawings he had collected over the war years. He included amongst them some pen and ink drawings of peaceful Italian villages and towns. He never painted or drew 'war scenes' or soldiers. "I don't know how war artists work, but sitting up in a slit trench in the middle of a battle was not for me. I kept my head down." As he was leaving Italy, he made barbed comments about the unpopularity of Winston Churchill amongst the troops. After six years he had had enough of war and army life. It was time to come home to Stockport.

'Italian Hill Village', *Water Colour, 1940s (Collection of Slim Ingram)*

Left Page (22): 'Italian Village', 12 x 9 inches, Oil on Canvas, 1940s (Private Collection)

'Florence', 7 x 9.5 inches, Pen and Ink/Water Colour, 1940s (Private Collection)

'Mrs. Clare's St. Bernard', *24 x 19.5, Pastel, 1945.* (Private Collection)

'Mrs. Clare's St. Bernard' was one of Alan's paintings soon after coming home from Italy. The picture was bought from the artist by a furniture dealer, Mrs. Jane Elizabeth Walker, who was a close friend of the painter, Helen Bradley. Her son, Michael Macintosh stated that, "On a number of occasions his mother had to comfort Helen after she had been disparaged by her husband, Tom, in his big booming voice, often in front of others. On one occasion Elizabeth had to take her for a long drive during which Helen sobbed uncontrollably after Tom had been particularly unpleasant."

'Fountain, Florence', *Water Colour, 1940s (Private Collection)*

Chapter 3 - Tom, Ron, Frieda - the late Forties and early Fifties

After the war, Lowndes returned a very different young man. He had seen much of the world on army service, and had been inspired by the treasures of Italy. What to do and where to do it? He may not have been aware of his immediate surroundings before the war, but he had now seen Africa, Rome, Venice and Florence. Stockport in the late forties was a grimy, dirty and smoky mill town. There was a post war boom and many fortunes were being made as a consequence. New engineering works started all around the town to supply the enormous post war demand. At the end of Church Road, where the Lowndes now lived, there was a busy engineering works, Hollis and Vine. Marion Demount in Stockport remembers well standing at the corner of the street and watching the mill girls returning home with all the fluff in their hair from the booming output in the textile mills. Chimneys belched smoke from domestic coal fires and industrial furnaces into the bowl of the valley and created dreadful smogs with a visibility of no more than a yard or two stifling breathing and covering clothing in an acrid dirty filth.

RIGHT: 12 CHURCH ROAD HEATON NORRIS

The Lowndes family lived here in Heaton Norris after moving from Oxford Street; it is almost opposite Christ Church School

Alan must have felt so like Frank Machin in the
looked from a hillside towards a depressing nor
have been Stockport of the late forties. Frank w
surroundings and especially with his landlady,
for Alan to return to his family, friends and the

Panorama of the 'smoky bowl' which was Stockport looking over the area once known as The Park towards Lancashire Hill across the Tame Valley. Faulders Mill is to the right, Lancashire Hill top left.

LEFT:

TWO VIEWS OF LANCASHIRE HILL, STOCKPORT. *Alan was to paint this street a number of times, including a powerful painting of the street to grieve over the barbarity of the council's demolition. (See over page)*

ABOVE RIGHT:

THE KING'S CINEMA, STOCKPORT, *where customers could bring their own 'seats'.*

He took the easy option and went back to his decorating job. Marion Demount recalls meeting him at the Church socials organised by the Reverend Peter Elfrick. Once a month on Saturday evenings these socials were held at the school (Christ Church), where records were played and everyone enjoyed old time dancing, the Gay Gordons and the Valeta, that sort of thing. Alan was the only member of the Lowndes family to attend. Marion remembers him vividly arriving dressed in a colourful velvet jacket and bow tie. "He was suntanned and had dark, almost jet black wavy hair, but the thing I remembered most of all was this lump on his head. It was probably a cyst or something like that, but as a young girl of about 11, I was intrigued. I thought he must be very brainy, or his brains were coming out of the lump".[5] She found Alan to be a rather nervy character and hopeless at dancing, "he used to just jump about without any sense of rhythm". She was in reality somewhat in awe of him.

It is rather surprising that his sisters Jenny and Christine never attended. Christine was a real beauty, "rather like Grace Kelly with lovely blonde hair shaped in a page boy style and a very beautiful complexion."[6] The two sisters were often to be seen in white tennis outfits on Saturdays in Masons shopping for groceries. Jenny in particular smoked very heavily. Sadly neither Christine nor Jenny was to enjoy a very happy life. Jenny became a serious alcoholic and died as a consequence of her drinking and smoking. Christine had three children, but was abandoned by her husband, Eric, a good looking man. She suffered from diabetes and lost a leg as a consequence.

DETAIL OF 'DESTROYING LANCASHIRE HILL', 20 x 30 inches, Oil on Canvas, 1966.
Formerly in the collection of the painter Fred Yates (Private Collection)

5 Marion Demount
6 Marion Demount

Fortunately, his sisters had shown Alan's 'Italian' drawings to Emmanuel Levy at the 'Tech', where he had enrolled before the war on the decorating course. Levy was impressed with the drawings, and said they were as good as any by the full time students on his course. Alan was able to enrol in an evening painting class under Levy's guidance. He had now joined the 'artists': he was no longer a mere decorator, a very important change of status. Some attest to a story that Emmanuel Levy once tore up one of Alan's drawings in front of the class, which made Alan even more determined to be an artist. The story is almost certainly apocryphal. In a letter to Alan dated 30-3-76, Emmanuel asked Alan to view his retrospective, where he "would see a photograph of the painting I did of you many years ago. It was presented to a museum in Israel and found a permanent place in a very lovely gallery." This is hardly an invitation from someone to whom Alan might feel ambivalent or antagonistic.

He also gave up his decorating job and gained employment in Frank's Studios in Manchester. Julius Frank, a German Jew, had escaped from Germany in 1933: he was a remarkable man. He had been an illustrator for the German army in World War I and after the war, he decided to study painting in Paris and then became a designer in Berlin. He had the good sense to foresee what was likely to happen to Germany with Hitler as Chancellor and fled to Britain. He came with nothing and succeeded beyond expectation. His design studios in 16 Oxford Street, Manchester soon became one of the most creative in the country; he also had a design studio in London. Frank made a great deal of money during the War: he once mentioned to Ron Thomas that he felt rather guilty that he should be making so much money, when others were being killed. Ron was a memeber of Julius's staff and later a good friend of Alan Lowndes. After the War, Manchester was full of French designers, who would come to the town to sell their original designs for fabrics or wallpapers to be finished in the many studios in the town.[7] Frank's was one of the only studios in Manchester to specialise in original designs, he never 'finished'. He sold his designs in many European countries, as well as in New York.

Julius Frank centre, Ron Thomas on his right, Julius's two sons left and right

Mr. Frank later married a German girl called Louise, who persuaded him to let her sell all his thirties designs around the Manchester area. Ron Thomas gave Julius a Lowndes painting as a wedding present. Frank was very much at the forefront of fabric and textile design in the area. He also contributed to the Palladio Scheme, a cutting edge selection of wallpaper designs produced for the architectural profession by Wall-Paper Manufacturers Ltd. in 1959.

---

7 *Ron Thomas: "The designs were brought over to Manchester to be sold to the printing firms. The term 'finished' in this context means the printing firm would work with the designs to enable them be put into 'repeat'. Once the 'repeat' had been produced then the engraving takes place and the "finished" design is printed."*

At Frank's studios Alan met Frieda Clowes with whom he became completely infatuated.[8] Ron Thomas, who also worked at Frank's described how he first met Alan. "I saw this attractive girl with a much smaller man draped all over her. I asked my friend who this extraordinary man was. 'It's Alan Lowndes', came the reply. I didn't see him again until some time later when he was on his own. Frieda had obviously given him up." Alan sometimes claimed that work in the studios was repetitive and somewhat dull, in reality it was quite stimulating. Apart from the attractions of Frieda Clowes, he was learning much about textile design from a real expert, who would help him considerably in his artistic development.[9]

RIGHT: *Frank's design and screen-printing staff - Standing - Alan extreme right, Frieda Clowes centre. Soon all except three were sacked, when Frank made losses in printing his own products*

Alan wrote that he was happy at Frank's painting headscarves. He found the iterative nature of the work enabled him to enjoy the actual process of painting. He painted directly onto the silk with brushes and dye colours. As a result of this work, he always liked to paint a subject that he knew so thoroughly, that he was able to concentrate totally on the actual application of paint to the canvas. He felt pleased that he could give a minimum obligation to any verbal thought to do with such a subject. "… and that is how I like to work. The best representational work always follows this rule."

As well as painting, he spent much time mixing socially with Ron Thomas and Tom Hassell. Ron had attended the Royal Salford School of Art during the War. Tom returned from the R.A.F. to take up a position as a draftsman. Both spent much time with Alan in the various pubs of the area. Ron usually found Alan happy with 'early doors' ending their visits at about 7 to 7.30p.m. He seldom talked about the war beyond his impressions of the art he had seen. He expressed leftish views in politics, but it was more the views of a 'have not', rather than serious political principle. Ron was painting political pictures of 'Dockers on Strike' or 'Speaker's Corner' at that time. They often discussed these types of topics. Ron felt that Alan liked the good things in life far too much to be a real socialist. Later Lowndes was to write in a letter. "I am a drop out from the social classes so I observe them, the workers still go their feckless way and so do most of the aristocracy but with increasing guilt and fear of the workers. However the good old middle twittering classes are always with us … Why do the middle classes work so hard at being dull? Were Thomas Hardy alive now, I'm sure he'd write. "And still she wanted a fitted carpet.""[10]

Tom was not quite so fortunate. He and Alan would often have late night sessions ending up with Alan staying at Tom's house. Tom's mother often used to berate Alan for being drunk and using her house as his home. Interestingly Tom was insistent that Alan never stuttered in his presence. Andras Kalman suggested his stutter eased in proportion to his drinking: when semi-drunk or drunk he was fluent, funny, always argumentative. Alan and Tom used to go fairly regularly to the Spanish Club on Wednesday evenings in Manchester, which is

8 Frieda briefly came into Alan's life again when she called into the Crane Gallery to ask after him in 1956. The gallery owner, Andras Kalman, wrote to Alan in France informing him of her visit.
9 The Victoria and Albert Museum holds one of Frank's designs printed by Simpson and Godlee, catalogue number 333-1953
10 Letter from Alan Lowndes to Elizabeth Horsfield, December 15th, 1977

where Tom met his charming wife, Antonia. On one occasion Alan came to London to stay with Ron, who was visiting Julius Frank's Hendon studio. Sadly Alan had a terrible habit of grinding his teeth somewhat loudly at night. At 2 a.m. Ron finally snapped and ejected Alan onto the London streets.

Tom, Alan and Ron often used to dispute artistic matters over their pints, though sadly Alan's love affair with Guinness had already become serious. He commented to Ron Thomas that he could live perfectly well on 'Guinness and fags'.

LEFT: 'TOM HASSELL', 18 x 13 inches, Oil on Canvas, 1949, (Private Collection)
MIDDLE: 'DANCING GIRLS' 24 x 19 inches, Oil on Card, 1952 (Collection of Ron Thomas)
RIGHT: *Alan Lowndes painting a portrait of Ron Thomas in his studio, Stockport*

The 'portrait' of Ron Thomas, 1950, in the photograph above right was the cause of a more serious quarrel. Ron had accused Alan of copying other artists, especially Matisse, as in the picture of 'DANCING GIRLS', above centre. Alan was furious and rubbed out his portrait in a rage. Ron was a little miffed, he had paid Alan for the canvas and a deposit for the portrait, money he never saw again. Both had perhaps forgotten Picasso's comment, "If there is something to steal, I steal it!"

Alan rented a studio in Bamford House in the Market Square in Stockport at a rate of 5 shillings a week, rising to 7/6d, though he could not afford it; he was blessed to have an accommodating landlord. His studio was on the top floor. It is thought that Stockport Market was the location of the last 'wife sale' in England. The wife sale apparently happened just down from the Market Place at the White Lion Hotel on Underbank in 1831, 'when one William Clayton sold his wife for five shillings to J. Booth, and she was handed over to the purchaser with a halter round her neck'. Ron Thomas vividly describes Alan's studio. "I went up these steep and rather dangerous stairs to the top floor. There was a door facing you, the toilet and two rooms on one side, a bedroom and his studio. The condition of the place was terrible, I don't know how he lived and painted up there. On the other side was another room rented by a painter who hadn't been there for a long time. Alan urged me to take over the room for my work. I decided at once I was not going to do this. I needed at least a meal a day at home. I simply could not work in this environment. Alan was amazingly productive considering his living and working conditions."

Diane Lovelock, widow of one of Alan's friends, Jim Lovelock, wrote to the author, "I wish I could remember some of the tales Jim told me about the unusual people who seemed to form a group and meet in this building. I know it had the nickname of "The Fornicatorium", but that's all I know and perhaps it is best not to know too much more!!!"

Detail of 'Stockport Market'. *17.75 x 22.25 inches. Oil on Canvas. 1949 (Private Collection, photograph by courtesy of the Crane Kalman Gallery) Alan's studio in the Market Square, Stockport, was on the top floor, first two windows on the main façade facing the square. This painting is more expressionist and bolder work with brush and palette knife.*

Ron continued, "Alan often used to play the recorder in his studio; he was really quite an accomplished player. He also loved reading poetry. One day he was reading poetry out loud to me in his studio, when he started to stutter. He gradually became more and more agitated and frustrated, until he finally threw the book away. Unfortunately he managed to throw it through his glass window."

'Sketch by Ron Thomas of Alan Lowndes playing his recorder in his studio, Stockport', *approximately 24 x 18 inches, Indian Ink on Paper, 1953*

It is very interesting to see the development of Alan's style during the late forties and early fifties. The paintings he sent to England from Italy during his army service appeared at this stage to be very much part of English watercolour painting, such as 'A: Street Scene, Florence'. Within a few years his style had completely altered through 'B: War Damage Assisi' to 'C: The Baker's Vaults' to become almost an Expressionist, a style that was to attract the art critic John Willett and the dealer Andras Kalman. (The three paintings are illustrated on the opposite page). In his autobiography Alan does not discuss his artistic influences at this time. He amusingly wrote in an early catalogue about his training as an artist, "Studied at Florence and Stockport." Ron Thomas, a fellow artist and close friend, is perhaps the best person to explain Alan's considerable change and development in these crucial years.

"Whilst Alan was working with Julius Frank, he was painting large splashes of bright colours for head scarves. He later went with all the unmarried staff to Belfast to design and paint large fabrics for the home. The staff learned to mix all the colours of their dyes and named the bottles with the colours, a practice very helpful to one member of staff, who was colour blind. The designs were bold, not at all intricate. It was the boldness of design that gave him the confidence to be a bolder painter.

In his studio in Stockport he covered the walls with cards of famous artists, especially Matisse, Chagall, de Chirico and the Fauves. The Fauves were an important influence for the Expressionists. He spent a lot of time copying these painters, a practice common to many young artists. He learned colour and composition from them, but gradually developed his own voice. He became especially skilled in the use of the palette knife for his oil paintings. One day I happened to be walking round my class of students, when I saw an open book and Matisse's picture of a girl wading was there. My God, I thought, Alan has copied this painting. I never mentioned to the students that my friend had copied this picture. In the same year he painted 'Back Alley Girl', which is much closer to his later style. You can see his understanding of his subject has really begun to develop.

A:

'Street, Florence'.
1944/45

B:

'War Damage, Assisi'.
8 x 16 inches, Oil on Canvas, Dated 1946 or 1947. (Private Collection) Signed ABL. In the early days he often included his middle initial, 'B' for Bailey. On this occasion he has simply signed with his initials.

C:

'The Baker's Vaults, the Pub with the Vicious Dog', near St. Petersgate in the Market Place, Stockport, 10 x 12.5, Oil on Canvas, 1948. The landlord's dog used to bite customers, hardly canine behaviour conducive to a profitable business. (Private Collection)

Detail of: 'Girl Wading', *Oil on Canvas, 24.5 x 29.5 inches, 1951.*

Detail of 'Back Alley Girl', *15 x 20 inches, Oil on Board, 1951*

Comment has been made about the tightness of his compositions. This did not come from his time at Frank's Design Studios. I think it came from the subject matter right in front of him. Stockport was made up of complex intertwining lanes and roads; he had to be tight to depict what he wanted. Also, as I have already said, he learned a great deal from his cards of the great painters. Gradually he developed his own colour and style to depict northern scenes, which at that time were rather complex, dark and dingy."

If any painting encapsulates Lowndes's transition from an 'English Water Colourist' to his more mature and expressive style, it is his early masterpiece, 'The Power and the Glory', 1949, 23 x 32 inches, Oil on Canvas, illustrated on pages 36 and 37. He could see the power station and town church (St. Mary's) from his studio window and decided to paint the two large buildings. He has depicted the power station, a building most of us would regard as rather ugly, as the attractive half of the composition with gentle reds, yellows and browns, whereas the church is much darker and looms over the painting from the right with its very slab like shape and darker colours. Perhaps he was having a slight joke or poking fun at the church and its pretensions. Even the dark church has considerable interest in its depth and subtle glow of colours and strong thick paint. The sky is a throwback to the English school of Constable through the Victorians to the twentieth century, but well painted and full of atmosphere. The power station and the area in front of it is full of luscious colours and impastoed paint, especially the wall in front of the power station. It is also one of his last paintings to be signed 'A.B. Lowndes'.

As ever with Lowndes, his composition is outstanding with the main shapes placed in exactly the right place to create the atmosphere he required. Particularly impressive is the contrast between the happy green fields and red wall of the power station 'half' with the more sombre greys and darker browns and ochres of the church 'half'. It is a painting that can only be fully appreciated in the 'flesh' and ought to be in a museum.

St Mary's Church

The Church has some interesting features. The burial ground contains the gravestone of John Wainwright, who composed the tune 'Stockport' to which is sung the hymn 'Christians Awake'. Every Christmas a memorial service for Wainwright is held at the church. Baptised here is judge John Bradshaw - the man who sentenced Charles I to death. An unknown hand has added 'traitor' to the Parish Register.

Right: 'Man and Dog', *13 x 9.5 inches, Oil on Canvas, Early Fifties (Collection of Ron Thomas)*

Pages Over (36-37): Detail of 'The Power and Glory', *23 x 32 inches, Oil on Canvas, 1949 (Collection of the Crane Kalman Gallery)*
Pages Over (38-39): Detail of 'Stockport Market Place', *15.5 x 21.5 inches, Oil on Canvas, 1949 or early 50s. (Private Collection)*

PREVIOUS PAGE: 'Stockport Market Place': "The subject of Mr Lowndes picture is the N.W. side of Stockport Market. All the buildings shown in the picture are still there. The building that looks like a church at the back of the picture is in fact the old Market Superintendent's Office in Castle Yard. Next to it on the left coming forward is the Baker's Vaults, an old Stockport pub, which is still going. The grey building in the middle with what looks like an old red telephone box outside is the Produce Hall, which still functions as such. It was built in 1851 of Yorkshire stone and has large classical columns at the front. It also originally housed the library on the first floor, but a new building was subsequently constructed for this purpose because the smells of the food, particularly cheese, coming up from the food hall below often became overpowering for the users. The other buildings housed various shops and businesses. These face the large glass Market Hall which dominates the centre of the Market Place and beyond that, in the N.E. corner is St. Mary's Church." Andrew Lucas, Stockport Heritage Library.

He was happy for a while at Frank's creating his own colourful and bold designs. He then made a rather unfortunate mistake, he left Frank's and set up in business with a partner he described as "a war wounded 'hero' who had been a 'spiv' and was still two thirds crooked. Being for the first time at least half my own boss - nearly unpaid - I had more time to paint … Eventually our 'business' ran into a near crooked mess. When it got hopeless (my partner had to flee the country) I decided enough is enough. This was the very early fifties. The army and the war had taught me that it is better to try to do what you want in life, because as far as I see you don't get another chance. As I wanted to be a painter, so I would be … I got a further number of canvases - mainly from junk shops - a lot of paint and pitched in. I didn't have an easel, just a cat ladder - the sort you lay along a roof to walk on - and I fixed a plank of wood to it."

Although Alan had left school at 14 and had not enjoyed formal tertiary education, he attended the best university of all, the university of books. Everyone has attested how widely he read, always ready with a quip or comment on almost any subject. Ron Thomas felt that the book that most influenced Alan was 'The Horse's Mouth' by Joyce Carey. He was hugely attracted to the bohemian lifestyle of Gully Jimson. He titled his sadly abbreviated unpublished autobiography 'The Confessions of a Provincial Bohemian'. It is fascinating that another important British artist, John Bratby, was also fundamentally affected by the same book. Writers have been unsure whether he was familiar with the so-called Kitchen Sink painters; he depicted grimy Northern scenes, they painted lavatories and dustbins. (See page 45, 'The Back Street')

There is a clue that he was fully aware of their work; in a letter to Andras Kalman he describes his visit to exhibitions in Paris in 1956. "In Rebeyrolle I saw nearly all of everything original that is contained in our English 'New Realists'. I would be ashamed on this count to go near the Venice Biennale next year. Rebeyrolle I need hardly add does it a lot better than Jack Smith, Middleditch or Bratby. If John Berger - who is a friend of John Willett's - does write on my show and does hail me as a New Realist I won't worry much, but at least I won't be under the 'original through Rebeyrolle' (who I like) classification."

REBEYROLLE, 'SELF PORTRAIT', 1952

At this time Rebeyrolle rejected the sophisticated tendencies of the School of Paris and attempted to scrutinise natural forms and develop his powers of drawing. He drew and painted what was round him, which was not at all 'beautiful' or 'pretty'; his atelier was situated amongst the slaughter houses of Vaugirard. His artistic style was to change in later life.

An exhibition of French realist painters at the Tate Gallery in 1955 had gained considerable popular acclaim and undoubtedly had an influence on the 'Beaux Arts Quartet', but did it influence Alan, especially the quasi-existentialist, Bernard Buffet, whose work he knew and admired? In 1956 P.A.T. reviewed Lowndes's Exhibition at the Crane Gallery with the headline, "The Dustbin School. Alan Lowndes is showing a selection of paintings … that are rich, individual, full of gusto and as honest as painting can be. They will give critics of 'dustbin painters' plenty to talk about". (Sadly the author has not been able to trace the identity of P.A.T.)

Ian Gale wrote in The Apollo Magazine in June, 1991: "Like the central character in Colin Wilson's 'The Outsider', Lowndes appears to be dabbling (one presumes unwittingly) with a form of existentialism." Gale continued: "Literary parallels abound throughout Lowndes's pictures, and the artist epitomises the cocky 50s optimism of Barstow, Braine, Waterhouse and Osborne. 'As we go through the gates into the streets,' wrote Barstow in a Kind of Loving (1960), 'a bint goes by on her stiletto heels.' Lowndes's young tarts encapsulate the seediness of Barstow, and not a trace to be seen here of the Victorian respectability of motherhood fixated Lowry. These are a young man's preoccupations: love, making of life for oneself, jazz bands, betting shops and pubs. Unlike the famous matchstick men, these are the solid figures described by Billy Liar: 'The fat women rolling along on their bad feet like toy clowns in pudding basins, the grey faced men reviewing the Sporting Pinks … Frowning women, their black scratched handbags crammed with half-digested grievances.' Here they all are captured by Lowndes.

In the Organ Grinder bloated housewives watch grubby children … playing in the street. Observed by a languid organ grinder two women chat in a door-way, defensively cross-armed, imbued with a profound sense of resignation and ennui. The window set in a red wall takes on a monumental significance, reflecting its importance in the daily life of the inhabitants of this mean little street. Like Hopper, the characters who inhabit Lowndes's townscapes themselves become loaded with dramatic content through their very lack of dynamism."

ABOVE: 'THE ORGAN GRINDER', 24 x 46 inches, Oil on Canvas, 1961 (Collection of the Crane Kalman Gallery)
OVER PAGE LEFT (42): 'THE PAWN SHOP', 36 x 27 inches, Oil on Board, 1955 (Collection of Cornel Lucas)
OVER PAGE RIGHT (43): DETAIL OF 'THE BACK STREET', 23 x 19 inches, Oil on Canvas, 1956 (Collection of the Crane Kalman Gallery)

Lowndes wrote in an unpublished article entitled 'Why we Paint' (1978), "I paint people and scenes which can be recognised as such, even if the accuracy can be disputed. I do not think that merely recording is the aim or job of the painter, and I have no interest in photographic detail - and very little in photography anyway." He said in an interview for B.B.C. North West Television in 1973, "A woman said to Matisse, 'You never see a woman with an arm like that'. He replied, 'It is not a real woman, it is a painting'." He used to make many sketches 'on the spot', but never painted there. He felt that it did not matter where he actually painted, his sketches and visual memory would be enough to complete whatever he was intending to do. As he said, "You rely on memory, your visual memory. If you haven't got a visual memory, you shouldn't be in the business."

Lowndes quickly developed a very fast method of painting. Ron Thomas stated that Alan could complete an oil painting in an hour or two using the wet on wet method, but this required great confidence and skill. When he produced a gouache, he would often use the medium as if it was oil or acrylic and layer it on thickly with an impastoed effect. It is quite difficult on occasions to differentiate between his gouaches and his oils, often leading later to mistakes in catalogues. He was fond of quoting Leonardo da Vinci's comment about artists having to study anatomy. "You learn it in order to forget it. The big rule in art is to know the performance of what you are using. Results are knowing the thing you are working with". These techniques learned early on in his career at Frank's and in his studio were to stay with him all his life. Above all he was developing his powers of observation, so crucial for his artistic development. He also said that when he began to paint, he never set out to baffle people; if he did so, then it was not his fault, he did not intend it.

'LET GO YOU BULLY', *11 x 14 inches, Oil on Board, 1949 (Collection of the Crane Kalman Gallery)*

'MIDDLE HILL GATE'. 20 x 18 inches, Oil on Board, 1954 (Collection of the Crane Kalman Gallery)

ABOVE TOP: 'PUB SCENE'. *21 x 28.25 inches, Oil on Canvas, 1952*
ABOVE 'SYLVAN GROVE'. *20 x 30 inches, Oil on Canvas, 1948 (Private Collection)*

RIGHT: 'THE ARCHES, STOCKPORT', 28 x 36 inches, Oil on Board, 1953 (Collection of the Crane Kalman Gallery)

'THE GASWORKS', 21 x 16 inches, Oil on Board, 1954 (Collection of Stockport Museum and Art Gallery)

OVER PAGE (48): DETAIL OF 'CHILDREN IN THE STREET', 30 x 25 inches, Oil on canvas, 1953 (Collection of Jim and Diane Lovelock) The young girl has a look so similar to the figure in blue in Poussin's marvellous 'Dance to the Music of Time' in the Wallace Collection. Did Alan see this picture?

'LUNATIC CAT', 22.5 x 18 inches, Oil on Board, 1953 (Collection of Jim and Diane Lovelock)
Jim Lovelock was a friend of Alan's in the Manchester/Stockport days. He agitated hard to persuade the council to block the demolition of the County Hotel in Stockport, alas to no avail. Please see Chapter 6 for further details of Lowndes's murals in the hotel.

'IN THE PARK', *54 x 77 inches, Oil on Board, 1950 (Collection of the Stockport Museum and Art Gallery)*

Chapter 4 - Elizabeth Horsfield and Andras Kalman (1919 - 1970)

The life of an impecunious artist was not easy for him in Stockport. Alan experienced a rather unfortunate time in his studio. No one had seen him for some time and assumed he had gone away. Eventually someone found him in a terrible physical state: his fingernails were said to be almost three inches long and his body was emaciated. he had almost starved himself to death. He was seriously ill and had to spend some time recuperating. Perhaps he was reincarnating Gully Jimson. This story also reinforced the prejudices of his immediate contemporaries towards him and artists in general. They were regarded as very strange, especially when word spread about some of their studio parties. A mystique of improper doings was created, which of course only made everything much more exciting to pass on to the next gossip. The life of an artist in parochial industrial Stockport was not an easy one.

He wanted to become a painter and achieve fame and hopefully fortune. but he was living in a society and time where "just about everyone assumed they would stay there all their lives ... There are two types of life: the first is the escalator life, where you move inexorably upwards, the other type is the carousel where you go round and round ... There are enough people making sure you stay on the carousel." (Richard Hoggart, 'The Uses of Literacy' published by Chatto and Windus and Penguin Books) There were all too many factors keeping him on the carousel, not least a new young woman, who was to play a major role in Alan's life.

'ELIZABETH HORSFIELD', 22.75 x 18.5 inches, Oil on Canvas, 1953. (Collection of Elizabeth Horsfield) Alan and Elizabeth were in his studio in Stockport chatting away while Alan quickly painted this portrait. In the early days Alan talked a great deal about Frieda Clowes, the 'love of his life'.

He met the most serious girlfriend of his life, Elizabeth Horsfield, who was to become his second 'love of my life'. Elizabeth was a trainee teacher at Didsbury Teacher Training College. Zena Doyle, a fellow student, suggested Elizabeth might like to meet a friend of hers, a twenty-eight year old painter, who was fun. Together with Zena and their friend Cynthia they duly met Alan. Her first impression was of slight amusement, especially 'how such a tiny fun man could be a painter'. Right from the beginning she knew their relationship was a non-starter, though she found him attractive, interesting and amusing. For Elizabeth, from a literate middle class home, this was a chance to start flexing her muscles in life, to be 'bohemian' in a relatively harmless way. They used to talk endlessly, or rather Alan talked all the time, which was always slightly difficult with his stammer. She was severely tempted to finish sentences, but never did so. They always met in his studio or in coffee bars, especially in the subterranean Kardomah café in Manchester's St. Ann's Square.

Alan affectionately called her Cilli (pronounced Chilly), because she reminded him of a Chinese actress and impersonator, Cilli Wang. He proposed marriage to her three weeks after meeting, but she did not want to be tied to Alan. For a few years they met many times to go to the theatre, concerts and of course coffee bars. She never discussed politics with Alan; she was more interested in literature and poetry. An extract from Dr. John Horsfield's (her younger brother) diary in 1953 illustrates the 'progress' of their relationship:

September 1st:	Betty told Alan a change in their relationship was needed.[11]
October 8th:	Alan and Betty went to Moulin Rouge
October 25th:	Betty went to see Alan
October 29th:	Alan came and attacked the R.A. (Royal Academy)
November 22nd:	Alan came after a row with Andras Kalman
November 24th:	Alan painting at the County Hotel[12]
November 25th:	Alan came with a cigarette holder.
December 12th:	Betty went out with Alan
December 18th:	John, Betty and Alan went to the cinema to see the Marx Brothers at the Circus …

John Horsfield commented that Alan used to look grey with fatigue. His parents wanted to help Alan and asked him to paint their kitchen, which he did on March 16th, 1953. In the end Elizabeth broke off their relationship, especially as she had met and fallen in love with Ray Boston, a B.B.C. journalist; they married in 1955. On the day of their wedding at St. Mary's Church, Nether Alderley, Alan turned up at Elizabeth's house and threw six large nude drawings of her on the floor and said, "They are unsigned and no use to me any more." The Bostons later left the drawings in a house in Kensington in 1955; the drawings have never been seen since. Incidentally, Ray was responsible for bringing Gardeners' Question Time to the nation. Alan was deeply jealous of Ray Boston. Sadly, Alan could not let Elizabeth go and would send rude comments to Ray's employers about Ray's probity. He even suggested to them that Ray had had sexual relations with Elizabeth when she was under age. All this was nonsense, of course.

ABOVE LEFT: *Elizabeth Horsfield aged 18, Manchester*

ABOVE RIGHT: *Elizabeth Horsfield aged 21, Stratford upon Avon*

11 In the Horsfield family Elizabeth was known as Betty
12 See Chapter 6 for further details of the murals he painted at the County Hotel, Stockport

'Pott Shrigley Farm'. *16 x 12 inches, Oil on Canvas, 1953 (Collection of the Artist) Pott Shrigley is a delightful hamlet located about one mile northeast of the small town of Bollington in northeast Cheshire. It is as rural as you can get with the buildings that form its centre huddled close to the top end of two valleys, overlooked by Holme and Nab woods on the higher ground and enjoying views of hills to the southwest. In all directions there are beautiful trees, fields, often with grazing sheep.*

'ALLEY CAT', 10 x 12 inches, Oil on Canvas, 1955 (Alan gave this painting as a present to Elizabeth Horsfield) 'Alley Cat' was featured in the B.B.C.'s Twentieth Century Antiques Road Show, 2005. Alan loved cats and included them in many pictures. It became quite a joke in the family, 'Where's the black cat in the painting?'

ANDRAS KALMAN
(1919-2007)

Meanwhile he had already met and established a special working relationship with a man, who was to shape his artistic life for the rest of his career. Andras Kalman, a Hungarian refugee during the war, had set up the Crane Gallery in a basement in Manchester in 1945. He had come to England to study leather technology at Leeds University and for a while was interned as a foreigner during the war. On his release, but still during wartime, he endured several menial jobs, especially at a tannery, where his hands were permanently dyed. After the war John Willett wittily stated that Andras fell inter alias in love with visual art.

Andras described his first contacts with Alan in 1950. "I was sitting in my gallery at lunchtime, when I noticed two young people enter. He had a rather beautiful face, high cheekbones, mop of hair, but bad teeth, alas. The girl was spectacularly attractive and a foot higher than he was, a blond girl. They seemed to come in every lunchtime. They were the only people I recollect that they looked at pictures and looked at the texture and how they were painted. They talked about the pictures, whereas 90% of the people, perhaps 99% of the people just walk round saying, 'I don't like this, I don't like that etc.', then they went out.

The pictures they liked I would be ashamed of today. I had borrowed them. They were the painters of Paris, the corniest painters, tourist painters. They painted Paris cafes, Paris cafes at night, Paris cafes with the lights on, the rain falling, women sitting under the awnings. I thought that might be an exhibition that could appeal in Manchester. Strangely enough Mr. Lowry came to that exhibition and bought a picture from me. He said to me "Well, and how is bus?" I said, "It is terrible." He said, "Well I like that little picture." On the floor there was a painting of a girl in a French park with a hat, the usual corny thing the people went to Paris to buy, well painted and take them back to Missouri or Michigan or wherever. He said, "How much is it?" "It is 16 pounds Mr. Lowry." "Oh, I would like to have it." He bought it and never hung it, and like so many other things it was on the floor. On his floor was a Freud drawing, Rossettis, he couldn't be bothered.

Anyway we persevered and one day this couple that used to come in at lunchtime and really look at paintings walked in, they fascinated me. I wondered, is he a writer, is he a musician, a painter maybe? As he looked so carefully at the paintings, it occurred to me that he is a painter. I never spoke to them a word. They were obviously tremendously in love. This little man who could sit in her lap like a baby, this big girl. They were then both textile designers.

Then one evening he came to the gallery on his own. To my surprise, with a terrible stutter, he said to me, "I, I, I, I, I, am a pppppppainter, wwwwwould you lllllook at mmmmmmy pictures?" He had an interesting face, not a moronic face as go to the football matches. I said "Yes, when?" He said, "If you have time, now." I had to lock up at about 6.30. I didn't even have a car. I asked him where he lived. He said, "Stockport." I had never been to Stockport. We went by bus and we got off near the market place. He took me up some rickety stairs to a room where there was no bed, only a mattress with a couple of blankets, and there were a dozen or so paintings, which obviously had been painted on old canvases, which he would use, they were cheaper than new ones.

I looked at these paintings. They fascinated me. I felt he had a genuine vision. We started to talk and had a pint in a pub. He said he had a reasonably tolerant landlord who didn't mind if he was late with the rent, 7/6d. He told me he went to art school at night. He had a tracing job and he had this glamorous girl. She wasn't a sophisticated glamour, she was the sort of woman that D.H. Lawrence would pick up. She was sensual, tall, easily laughing. All I can remember her name was Frieda (Frieda Clowes). I told him I was having an exhibition in about three weeks time. This was 1950, I had opened in December 1949. I was to have an exhibition of Lucien Freud, John Craxton and two others in April (1950). I asked Alan how many pictures he had. He said, "Maybe 12 or 15." I told him that in the little niche near my desk in the gallery, there was room for about 6 or 7 pictures. He was absolutely delighted. I told him he was going to hang with two very sophisticated London painters, who were always having drinks at the Ritz hotel, and one of them (Freud) was going out with Lady Caroline Blackwood, who later committed suicide. Freud dressed like a male model with his hair beautifully coiffured.

I got the exhibition from a London Gallery, which was run by a very old hunchback refugee lady. She had connections with the English surrealist, Penrose, who with Magritte was trying to interest the English in surrealism and hard-edged realism of Freud and Craxton. I asked the Manchester Guardian critic to see the exhibition. The paper had already published a favourable review of my first exhibition, which was a terrible mixture of Epstein, Sir Gerald Kelly and Augustus John drawings etc.. Nobody was buying anything. My next exhibition was borrowed from Gimpel Fils, lithographs by Picasso and Braque. For £22.00 you could buy a Picasso of an edition of 50 or 75, which today would probably be worth £50,000.00.

My third exhibition was this one with Craxton and Freud; both are still alive hating each other. I smuggled in Alan Lowndes. The Guardian critic at that time was one of the youngest intelligence officers in the British army during the war, John Willett, who stayed a friend of Alan until he died. He was one of those English people who looked as if they were just putting a few pence together to get by. He was a descendant of the estate agents, Willetts with a huge place in Sloane Square. He dressed very shabbily and was a very intelligent man. He had been sent behind enemy lines with Popski as a sort of extra mural person with the army and wrote the book on Popski's Private Army.[13]

He wrote that Craxton and Freud were something like Bond Street sophisticates or Bond Street trendies, something like that. He then stated that though their paintings were technically accomplished, Lowndes the son of a railway worker had something to say, encouraging things like that. I sold one Freud for £70.00. That gave me quite a lot of encouragement. John Willett was writing a book on German Expressionists, and Alan Lowndes's early pictures were almost like early Kirchners, crude. In England crudeness, filthiness and rudeness is going down well under the leadership of Mr. Saatchi. In those days crudeness was the same as somebody being unable to paint."

Erica Pugh and her mother attended that exhibition. Erica, an art student had met Alan occasionally at the Kardomah Milk Bar. She recalled that Alan 'always seemed to be in the need of a good wash'. Her mother spent time talking to Alan and was captivated by him. She also liked the colours in 'War Damage, Assisi' and bought it for her husband. (Illustrated on page 33.)

RIGHT:
'THE CRANE GALLERY, MANCHESTER', *16 x 20 inches Oil on Canvas, 1952 (Collection of the Crane Kalman Gallery)*

---

13 Popski: 'A Life of Lt. Col. Vladamir Peniakoff' by John Willett. Peniakoff or 'Popski', as he was known, was the commander of a small wartime force known as Popski's Private Army.

THE GUARDIAN
MANCHESTER, SATURDAY,
April 1, 1950

BITTER AND MILD

Of the five painters exhibiting this month at the Crane Gallery, Manchester, the most interesting are not Freud and Craxton, the stars of the show, but Stephen Gilbert and Alan Lowndes. Gilbert is an Irishman with obvious gifts—an excellent sense of lively, clear colour and a fluent, calligraphic line—which he squanders on small, symmetrical, witty fantasies that in their general conception are reminiscent of Kubin. If he tackled something harder and more substantial he could paint pictures really worth looking at. (A sense of humour is not necessarily lost in making a major effort—look at Brueghel.) Lowndes, in contrast, has a definite approach and feeling, and this comes out both in the subtle colour and plasticiney texture of his paint and in the general atmosphere of his best pictures—"The Pub," say, or "Sylvan Grove."

These are successful and highly personal, in spite of their weaknesses—the sometimes dubious composition, the odd lapse of colour, and the still unpractised figures. He is a local painter, and this is his first show.

As for the rest, Allan Milner seems to be entirely on the wrong track, lacking as he does the verve of Picasso, the balance and colour-sense of Ben Nicholson, or the fascinated sense of form of early cubism. Without these things abstract painting becomes just pointless. John Craxton does some pleasant Picassograms, and his straightforward chalk drawings are good; generally, however, his work seems neither to pose nor to set any serious problems. Nor does the slick yet sensitive work of Lucien Freud. Both these latter have been strongly supported by the highbrow literary monthlies, and one can only take their judgment as a measure of the feebleness of criticism in our day. J. W.

JOHN WILLETT, *The Guardian*, April 1st, 1950

'THE MARKET PLACE', 48 x 72 inches, Oil on Board, 1953 (Collection of the Crane Kalman Gallery

LEFT PAGE LEFT:

DETAIL OF 'GUINNESS GIRL'. *14 x 11.5 inches, Oil on Board, 1950*

LEFT PAGE RIGHT

'MUM SWEEPING'. *16.5 x 12.5 inches, Oil on Canvas, Early Fifties (Collection of Ron Thomas)*

LEFT:
'GIRL STANDING'. *Oil on Canvas, 17.5 x 15 inches, 1948. Please note, the painting has been signed ABL. (Collection of the Crane Kalman Gallery)*

'WALKING DAY'. *48 x 72 inches, Oil on Board, 1956 (Collection of the Crane Kalman Gallery)*

LEFT: DETAIL OF 'LANCASHIRE HILL'. *12 x 15 inches, Oil on Canvas, 1950 (Collection of Nicholas Horsfield)*

DETAIL OF 'STOCKPORT STREET SCENE'. *21.5 x 17.5 inches, Oil on Board, 1953 (Collection of the Crane Kalman Gallery)*

PAGE RIGHT (61): 'Stockport Mill', *24 x 20 inches, Oil on Canvas, 1953 (Collection of Ron Thomas)*

LEFT: 'WASH NIGHT', 15.5 x 12 inches, Oil on Canvas, 1954. The painting has also been incorrectly titled 'Friday Night'.

LEFT: 'SEATED NUDE', 20 x 16 inches, Oil on Canvas, 1953 (Collection of the Crane Kalman Gallery)

'TWO WOMEN WALKING', 21.75 x 13 inches, Water Colour, 1957 (Collection of Bill Clark)

Alan and Andras were to develop a friendship that went much further than the dealer/artist relationship. Andras must have seen something of himself in Alan, they were the same diminutive size, both were in a sense outsiders struggling with nothing to succeed against the odds. Alan came from a slum in Stockport, Andras was a Hungarian refugee, who had come to study before the war, but was interned for a while as an enemy alien. Later in the war he made many walks through the slum terraces or 'ginnels and snickets' of Bolton on the way to work in a tannery and could empathise with Alan's street scenes. Andras took a bold step indeed to start the Crane Gallery in a basement in Manchester. He was saved financially in the early days by his excellence in tennis; he had been one of the top junior players in Hungary; he was soon asked to coach. "I made more money out of tennis coaching than I did in the gallery."

Alan had by now decided to become a full time painter. However short of money he may have been at many times in his life, he never abandoned his chosen career of earning his living entirely as a painter. After the exhibition Alan helped with odd jobs in the gallery and running errands, he even took the typewriter to be pawned on Friday, when times were really bad. Alan was particularly pleased when Andras was able to substitute an expensive watch, which wasn't so heavy; the pawnshop was a long bus ride away. He had the good sense to see that Kalman was "playing for keeps, not for fun like the other galleries in Manchester."

Life was not always smooth for Alan and Andras in their day-to-day dealings. Alan wrote a long and peppery six page letter from his Church Road house to Andras on July 19th 1952 or 1953 complaining about the way he was being treated, especially the manner in which Andras ticked him off in front of other people. Both his ending and the envelope would suggest that Alan's sense of humour prevailed.

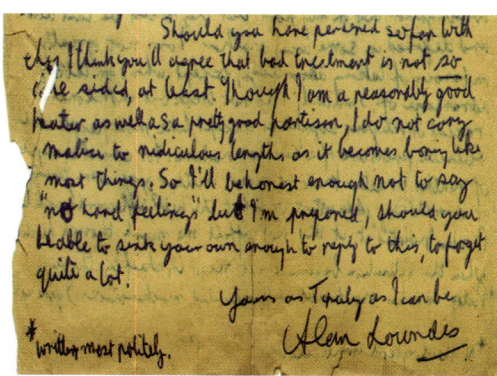

Whatever Alan may have thought when he was at a low ebb, he had achieved something other young artists in the area dreamed about, a gallery to represent him. Andras had sold hardly any of his paintings, but soon was to buy some of them himself. Ron Thomas was present when the deal was done and gave the following account of what occurred. "Andras had a backer for the gallery, Joe Braka. There were 12 or 15 paintings, I can't remember how many exactly propped up along the walls of the gallery. Joe and Andras were whispering together to decide on a price for the lot. After a while Joe said "£200.00 or £100.00." I can't remember the figure. Alan immediately said, "I'll have it, thanks." I told him to wait a moment, and asked the two of them to allow us to discuss the offer. We went outside, and I impressed on Alan the need to argue about the price and not accept the first figure. But no. Alan said he needed the money and was going to take what was on offer. The deal was struck. Alan was paid and we went to the pub. The whole time we were there, Alan complained that he had been robbed and should have been paid more."

Ron Thomas commented that he and Alan gained a great deal from the many different works being shown at the Crane Gallery. "Graham Sutherland, Ivan Hitchens and Henry Moore, wonderful painters and sculptors such as these were regularly passing through the gallery. Normally we could only view them from afar at galleries, but we could actually handle a Moore sculpture. This was magic indeed for us. On one occasion, Andras was driving us in a small car he owned. Alan and I were in the back, and a Moore sculpture of a head was on the front seat. It was a wet evening. As we turned from Market Street to drive towards the gallery, the door flew open and the statue went bouncing down the road. Andras was distraught. Eventually he managed to have it repaired."

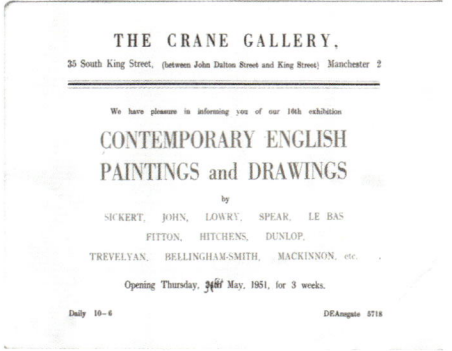

Alan has drawn a rather charming nude study on the back of one of Kalman's invitations for a mixed exhibition, May 31st, 1951

Alan was also fortunate to have met two other men, who were to prove important in his career and life. John Willett had commented on the exhibition and soon became a friend. Nicholas Horsfield, a very promising painter came to Manchester from London to work for the Arts Council. He knew John Willett and Andras Kalman, and through them met Alan, who fascinated him as a character. Everyone thought that Nicholas had at his disposal considerable largesse from the Arts Council; in reality he was paid a humble wage and could only influence and advise, certainly not grant any money. Nevertheless, Nicholas soon was able to pass on his many contacts to the artists of the area and act as a focal point for matters artistic.

Nicholas was amused and intrigued by Alan. "He didn't care a cuss about anybody, it was so refreshing. He was well read, but not at all the normal didact. He could tune into any conversation, turn it round, and we would all roar with laughter. An example of this is shown when Andras Kalman and his friends were having a serious discussion in a coffee shop about the mass murderer, Christie. At a moment of silence Alan suddenly said, 'All I cccccc can say about this fellow Ch Ch Ch Christie is that he had a very qu qu qu qu quiet taste in women.' We all laughed."

Nicholas was especially intrigued by Alan's disregard for convention. Andras had been buying and selling attractive tourist 'Paris' pictures. Alan thought this was a great idea and wondered how he could benefit. He came up with an amusing solution - suddenly there appeared a French artist, Andre Lobaire, who painted pretty little flower pieces, which the gallery sold for 10 guineas. This went on for a year or two, before Alan became bored with the whole idea. He went to John Willett and asked him if he could write an obituary for Andre Lobaire. John, a first rate scholar, was outraged at this suggestion and sent him packing. Alan then went to the Arts Council representative, Nicholas Horsfield and proposed the same story. Nicholas also refused to have anything to do with it. Alan just could not understand why his two friends would not help him. It is not known how Andre Lobaire finally met his end. As Alan wrote in his unpublished article 'The Day I died', "Andre Lobaire died the same day I did. His death and the manner of it remains a mystery to this day. In St. Ives I was suffering only a broken heart or kidney or liver or something. Lobaire was a famous painter. His birth was also a mystery."

At this time art life in towns like Manchester and Liverpool centred round Kardomah milk bars or pubs, and in Lowndes's case normally the latter. "The pubs did not take kindly to it, but the cafes largely ignored it." He was often in discussion with left wing intellectuals like John Willett and claimed he never met any other kind of intellectual. He received the usual lecture that he couldn't be a communist unless he painted abstracts. Firstly he never wanted to be a communist, and secondly he tried to paint in the abstract manner, but failed. His group centred their arguments on the necessity of bringing art to the people. As he said, "I felt that my painting would be more comprehensible to them than, say, the latter day Mondrian." Unfortunately the 'people's' reaction to his paintings was predictable. Those that viewed his work regarded his paintings as efforts their children could easily surpass. Alan Tucker, Sam Junior's friend and an amateur artist was somewhat reluctantly taken to see Alan's pictures. He was appalled by what he saw, "They were so child like."

FLOWERS IN A JAR, *24 x 10.5 inches, Oil on Board, 1960.*

Andre Lobaire would have been proud of this painting.

Lowndes constantly had to explain himself along the following lines:

"Oh, so you are an artist."
"Yes"
Then comes the bit about the son, daughter, sister, uncle, aunt, who does water colours and has been hung in the Royal Academy or is good at arranging flowers.
"Are you a commercial artist?"
"No"
"Ah, you teach in art school?"
"No, I just paint pictures."
"What kind?"
At this point he sometimes said, "Plain and coloured but mostly coloured."
"Not abstract?"
"No"
"Is that all you do?"

He vividly described the pain and horror on the faces of parents of various girl friends after such a conversation. As he said, "It leaves its mark on a man."

Nicholas Horsfield was in contact with most of the young artists in the Manchester and Liverpool area. He commented that Alan didn't really mix in the local art world at all; he was in the unique position of having a gallery to represent him and was the envy of other artists. Alan often portrayed himself as a working class socialist, yet he could never make friends with another leading working class painter in Liverpool, Arthur Ballard. In fact Ballard almost detested Lowndes, whether through jealousy or personal animosity is not known. Arthur Ballard was skilled in picking quarrels with other artists. He even came to blows with the sculptor and character, Arthur Dooley.

Fortune smiled about two years after the Freud, Craxton, Lowndes exhibition. The Crane Gallery was holding a Lowndes one-man show, when three gentlemen came into the gallery and said they liked the pictures. Andras was delighted that someone at last approved of the paintings. They asked him how much the pictures cost. "£5 to £15." "We would like to buy about eight or ten." "What!" "We would like to buy eight or ten." They went round looking at the paintings to make their selection. It turned out that two of the men were the Boulting twins, who had just filmed 'I'm All Right Jack'. The third member of the group was Sidney Bernstein, later Lord Bernstein. Alan and Andras thought they were going to be rich, and for both of them it was the beginning of a long association with film stars, directors and writers.

Andras used the proximity of the Palace Theatre to his gallery to make as many contacts as he could with the leading actors and producers. The visit of the Boulting brothers and Sidney Bernstein had given the gallery great impetus. Kalman soon worked out that actors had a great deal of spare time before evening performances, so he would invite them to spend a few moments viewing paintings in his gallery just down the road (about an eight minute walk). He always made sure he telephoned the press to arrive at the same time as the 'celebrities'. He asked Michael Redgrave to open an exhibition, he readily accepted. Soon most of the leading actors became friends and clients. Charles Laughton, Richard Attenborough, Albert Finney, the Steigers, Mai Zetterling, Michael Parkinson and many others became collectors of Lowndes's paintings. Laughton told Andras 'he had found a Modigliani of the streets.'

Of all the famous actors, Laughton and his wife Elsa Lanchester became good friends. Laughton was born to the proprietors of the Victoria Hotel in Scarborough just before the turn of the century. His parents wanted him to take over the business, and Charles briefly trained at Claridge's Hotel in London. However, after serving in the war, he settled in London and pursued his first love, acting. He became widely known for his strong performances in films such as 'Mutiny on the Bounty' and the 'Private Life of Henry VIII'. He also loved art and acquired a large collection of paintings. In 1929 Laughton married Elsa Lanchester, who appeared to condone his homosexuality. There was both a loving and farcical quality to the marriage, which the couple often brought to roles together on screen.

Elsa Lanchester had gained great acclaim for her role in the Bride of Frankenstein. She is also remembered for two famous quotations. "She looked as though butter wouldn't melt in her mouth . . . or anywhere else." And, "I thought she was a Method Actress. Afterwards somebody informed me that she was merely a manic-depressive." Elsa mentioned Lowndes many times in her autobiography, in which she wrote that Alan was so poor, he could not afford brushes and had to use a knife. No doubt Alan's mischievous sense of humour was involved in this statement forgetting the palette in front of knife. On one occasion the Laughtons asked him to join them for dinner at the very posh Midland Hotel. Alan of course turned up in his scruffy clothes and could not persuade the doorman or waiters to let him in. Luckily Elsa saw what was happening and told the staff not to worry, the scruffy little man was their guest. Some years earlier in 1904 Mr. Royce had met Mr. Rolls in the same hotel.

This was not the only time Charles Laughton invited Alan to a swanky dinner. In 1956 he asked him to join Elsa and himself for dinner at the Savoy to celebrate the opening of the 'Lowndes Gallery' in Laughton's home in Los Angeles. Somehow Alan managed to persuade his former girlfriend, Elizabeth Boston (Horsfield/Cilli), to join him leaving her husband to look after the baby on a particularly smoggy evening. The baby cried all evening. Interestingly, later on Elsa wrote to Lowndes on June 14th, 1973 referring to the 12 paintings she owned. "I get them out and also show them to people very often. But they're not hung around the house for this reason: Stockport and California sunlight are so different that the paintings don't really look at their best here. They need the low sun of England." She also suggested in the letter that he must have become prosperous by now - if only.

'THE ACTOR'
(CHARLES LAUGHTON),
24.5 x 19 inches,
Oil on canvas, 1958
(Collection of Betty
Goldfield, formerly
collection of Charles
Laughton)

'A CUP OF TEA. ELSA LANCHESTER (STANDING) AND JOYCE REDMAN (SITTING)', 30 x 22 inches,
Oil on Canvas, 1958 (Collection of Betty Goldfield, formerly Collection of Charles
Laughton)

'THE D'JANGO CLUB, MANCHESTER'. *20 x 16 inches, Oil on canvas, 1958 (Collection of Betty Goldfield, formerly Collection of Charles Laughton)*

LEFT: 'THE KISS', 24 x 16.5 inches, Oil on Board, 1958 (Formerly in the collection of Charles Laughton)

The Kiss was one of the paintings bought by Charles Laughton and his wife, Elsa Lanchester. Lowndes greatly admired the work of Gustav Klimt, and there is no doubt his picture was inspired by Klimt's 'The Kiss' 1907/08. Alan painted another version of this picture, which is in the collection of Ron Thomas. Ray Boston considers 'The Kiss' to be a grudge against him for 'stealing' Alan's girl friend, Elizabeth, hence the two figures depicted are Alan Lowndes and Elizabeth Horsfield.

Lowndes always wanted to communicate with people. "It is probably this sense of an artist performing through his work is what makes his pictures appeal so particularly to people in the theatre and cinema. Oddly enough he has never done anything to speak of in the theatre himself ... He has done a number of paintings on circus and fairground themes (though none, so far as I can remember, of the theatre proper), but the pictures collected by his theatrical patrons have mostly been scenes from Stockport street or pub life. The fact is, perhaps, that he paints them like a skilled producer, picking the right cast, giving them only the essential props, and grouping them expressively in front of an evocative set."[14] Charles Laughton told Lowndes his paintings were 'good theatre'. Alan himself thought that "Artists are good at setting the scene and the movement. I am sure this is the bit that appeals to the actors in my paintings."

The times were right for the working class painter. Books such as Room at the Top or Billy Liar, "the new underground novels of John Wain and Kingsley Amis, and just over the horizon the yelps and growls of John Osborne's Look Back in Anger",[15] but especially films such as This Sporting Life, A Taste of Honey, A Kind of Loving and I'm All Right Jack changed the pre war atmosphere completely. Suddenly it was fashionable to write about, photograph and paint the working classes, their aspirations, hopes and daily lives. The T.V. soap that was to become the great window on the working class world was inspired by a painting by Lowndes entitled 'Coronation Street, Stockport'. Tony Warren its creator worked at one time for Andras Kalman. He admitted in a Russell Harty T.V. programme that the idea of calling his programme 'Coronation Street' had indeed come from Lowndes's painting, 'Coronation Street, Stockport'. (Illustrated on pages 72 & 73) Tony's employer, Sidney Bernstein, the head of Granada Television, owned several of Alan's paintings.

Willis Hall and Keith Waterhouse became particularly good friends and admirers of Alan's work. In the fifties, Colin Welland, then an art teacher also became a good friend. He used to tell Alan that his technique was all wrong. "We met regularly in the jazz club (D'Jangos).

14 & 15 John Willett

I treated his work with scorn. I told him he had leap-frogged the basics and would get nowhere until he mastered draftsmanship." At an opening in the 70s, a more affluent Colin Welland admitted to Valerie Lowndes, when he met her for the first time, "If only I had understood Alan's work then."

Andras Kalman commented to the author, "In the film, A Taste of Honey, Tony Richardson and his cameraman Walter Lassaly used Alan's painting, The Power and the Glory, to create the scene where Rita Tushingham is consoled by a charming young man after the loss of her child - the bench on which she was sitting, the black church and the fields beyond - all straight from the painting." To complete the Crane Gallery story, Andras Kalman acquired premises in Knightsbridge, London, for his new gallery to be named the Crane Kalman Gallery. One of his first exhibitions was for Alan Lowndes in 1957 entitled 'Alan Lowndes of Stockport'. This was little different to the Crane Exhibition of 1956 - see pages 80 to 83. He continued the Crane Gallery in Manchester for a while with employed staff, Reg and Pamela. 'The staff' and Lowndes had many conflicts necessitating long letters from Lowndes to Kalman explaining matters.

John Willett wrote an introduction for the Crane Kalman Gallery exhibition of Alan's works, 'Alan Lowndes of Stockport 17th October - 2nd November 1957' in which he sounded a few words of warning. "He ought to be content with his present position: he has it in him to achieve much more: and if he practised with, say, the application of a musician he could do it. His drawing and composition are simply not careful enough, and he ought to have enough faith in his own talents to get them right (as much duller people can do) . . . the more one realises that it is not necessarily the most gifted who make the great painters; it is those determined to make the best use of their gifts." Future events would show whether John Willett was right in his assessment of Lowndes's art in the early fifties. It is also interesting to note the importance given by critics of the time to the quality of drawing, somewhat different to today, when artists with little drawing ability or even talent are grotesquely praised.

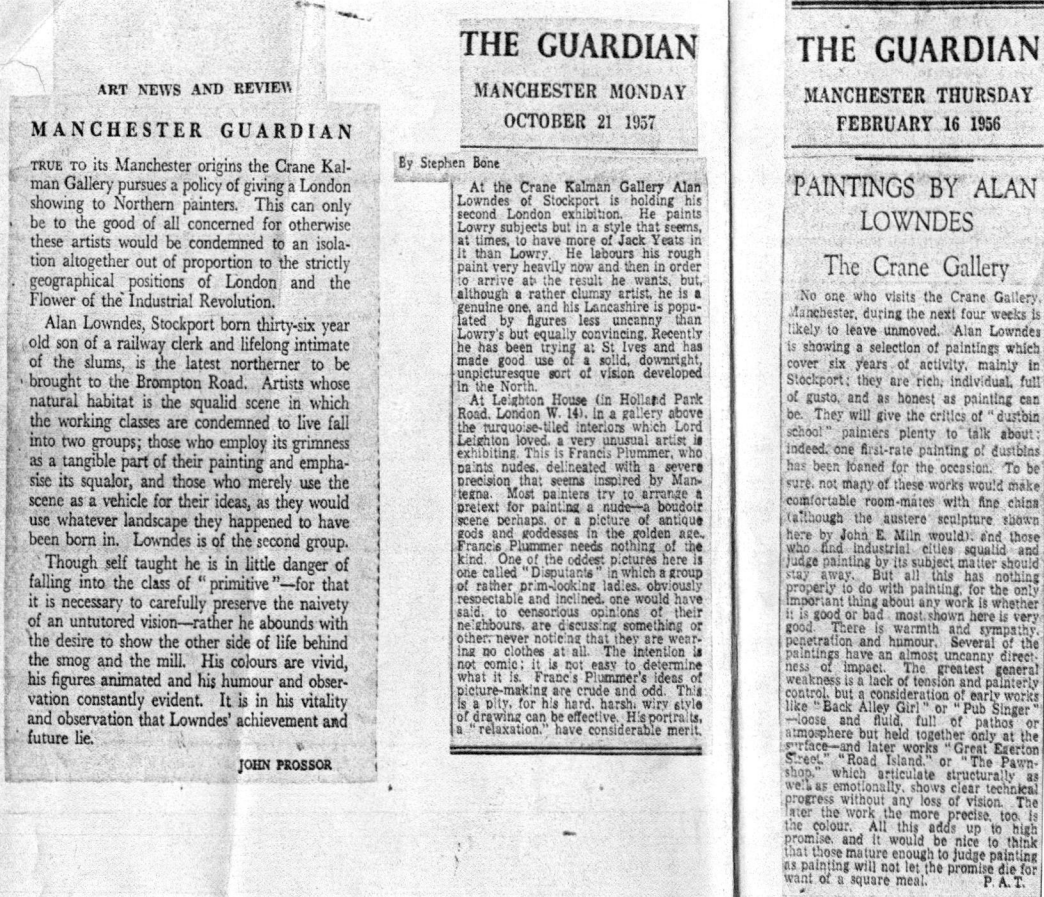

Various Press comments from the Guardian in the mid fifties

PAGES OVER (72-73): DETAIL OF 'CORONATION STREET, STOCKPORT', 28 x 36 inches, Oil on Board, 1961 - the painting that inspired a thousand 'soaps'. (Private Collection, photograph by courtesy of the Crane Kalman Gallery)

LEFT:
Cover of Alan Lowndes's first exhibition in London in 1957 at the Crane Kalman Gallery.

RIGHT:
Michael McNay succinctly stating the attraction of Alan's paintings to the media. The Guardian, 1968

MIDDLE LEFT:
Alan with Jo Grimond, then the leader of the Liberal Party, the Crane Kalman Gallery, date unknown.

MIDDLE RIGHT:
Alan and the actor Albert Finney at the Crane Kalman Gallery, date unknown

Alan with the actor David Tomlinson during his Retrospective Exhibition at the Stockport Art Gallery, November 28th, 1972

Chapter 5 - St. Ives

Needless to say, Alan was still always short of money, even after his initial successes. He worked for a while as a scenic artist at the Palace Repertory Theatre, Sale, when he had ambitions to become a stage designer, and needed a reasonably steady but minimal income to take out one of his few 'steady' girlfriends; he always pursued distinctly middle class girls. "It is strange, he never had any money, and they really took him out. A repertory company at that time had about 20 flats. On a Saturday night they would take them down and re-erect them in a different order to have doors and windows in different places for the next production. The scenic painter had to work like mad at the week-end to change the colours. That wasn't Alan. He was trying to get out of the rut his family was in, the rut was Stockport; he wanted to get out of Stockport. In many ways he was born out of his time. If he had appeared ten or fifteen years later, say the sixties, he would have been part of the scene. Things were not going too well for him at the Crane Gallery, at that time, as he described it, "A brash young painter was having a show there."[16]

He hated his job at the Palace Theatre; he also claimed in his autobiography the last straw was listening to rehearsals in R.A.D.A. trained posh voices. Slim Ingram considers Alan to have made this up after the event. When he was painting the stage flaps, there were no actors present. Slim feels that the three boys, Sam, Colin and Alan inherited their resentment of the middle and upper classes from their father, Sam Senior, who was very much the trade unionist in his job and life. Colin appeared to be the least affected. On the other hand, it must be remembered at that time in the North, speaking even standard English was suspect; it was talking 'well-off'. The chip he had about the middle classes was very much part of his psyche, unless they were females. Lowndes had a theory about girls. "One thing that attracted me to middle class girls is that they are pretty good in bed being well fed as a rule and that they know about comfort not luxury (but that is for the workers and Lords and Dukes etc.)."[17]

In the summer of 1955 Lowndes made his first trip to St. Ives. He wanted to get away from Stockport and Manchester, which is hardly surprising, as he continually had to explain himself. He had heard of the art scene in Cornwall from other artists, though this could not have been a major influence; he had tended to avoid other artists. Ron Thomas tells an amusing story about a discussion they had on the way to the bank on a wet spring day in 1952. Joe Braka in the Crane Gallery asked Alan and Ron to bank about £250.00 cash for him. They turned right out of the gallery and right again into a short 'tunnel' under the shops before arriving at King Street. In the tunnel Alan turned to Ron and said, "Why don't we just take the cash and move down to St. Ives in Cornwall." Ron quickly disabused him of the idea, which was certainly a joke, but it does indicate that Alan was aware of the town and county even in 1952.

Far and away the most important and only real reason for his journey to St. Ives was the break up of his somewhat one-sided relationship with Cilli, the love affair was over and Alan was distraught. In a letter to Cilli many years later he wrote, "I went to Cornwall with Land's End and suicide in view. How I got sidetracked into St. Ives is a long story. For a year I cared about naught for anyone or anything. When I came out of it at the end of that, I realised I had tried to hold love down underwater until its last wriggle and - I thought - final death."

Lowndes's relationship with and rejection by Elizabeth Horsfield (Boston) was a fundamental factor in his psychology and state of mind. He had never really known his mother and had thus never enjoyed a mother son relationship of any kind; as a consequence, he found it difficult to relate fully to women. He also felt all women he cared about rejected him, starting with his mother's premature death, then Frieda Clowes, and now Elizabeth Horsfield at a time when he was already relatively old, being thirty-four. He was unable to have a loving relationship again for some years, until he met and fell in love with his wife, Valerie. It would be interesting to surmise if his excessive drinking and pub centred life would have developed as it did, if Elizabeth had accepted him, and, he had had someone he cared deeply about to come home to in the evenings. In his own family there was a propensity towards alcohol; Elizabeth's rejection gave him a major nudge towards accelerating his love affair with the demon that would kill him in the end. This episode

---

16 Slim Ingram
17 Alan Lowndes in a letter to Elizabeth Horsfield 15th December, 1977

was undoubtedly the major factor of his formative years and crucial in exacerbating his alcoholic lifestyle.[18]

Throughout his life Alan found it very difficult to accept Cilli had rejected him in favour of Ray Boston. Even as late as 1977 he was writing to Cilli, "Every time I have a show somewhere I get a crop of letters and phone calls, mostly from Ex's from the old Manchester days. Not that I include you amongst these, you were the Ex ... why have they all been jealous except you? I suppose one answer is that I was in the incongruous position of being the older man competing with the not only younger but better off man: in that he had a regular job which I have still have not got." Lowndes could never accept that Cilli had fallen in love with another man and not with him. Ray Boston and Elizabeth (Cilli) were married on August 6th, 1955. Alas Cilli died in 2005; Ray Boston wrote, "She died in my arms, choking on a piece of toast, 11.00 a.m. September 21, 2005. She had been suffering on and off since the age of sixteen with multiple sclerosis."

St. Ives was incidental; Cornwall had the great attraction of being as far away from Manchester as it is possible to be without going abroad. He had already tried living in London and visiting Soho, Chelsea and the usual bohemian scene without being seduced to stay. Alan had written to Andras Kalman announcing his likely departure and commented about his drinking in an oblique way. Clearly Andras had earlier urged him to reduce his intake. Money and alcohol were to remain constants in their lengthy correspondence.

Undated letter from Alan to Andras sent from his family address of 12 Church Road, Stockport announcing his impending departure and his desperation.

---

18 There has been much confusion over the date of Alan's first visit to St. Ives. Kalman stated in his introduction to 'Paintings by Alan Lowndes', 1956, that he spent the summer of 1955 washing up there. All documentary evidence and dates of paintings would suggest this was indeed the first time he went.

Alan drew a rather charming cartoon of Andras Kalman on the back of an undated letter, probably written in 1955.

At least Lowndes could comfort himself with the weather being warmer and cleaner than cold smoggy Stockport, and he might meet more like-minded artists. He was also very fortunate to have found a sponsor for his first year in St. Ives, Mr. Crabtree of Hebden Bridge, who 'out of the goodness of his heart' sent him £10.00 per month. Thomas Crabtree had bought a number of paintings from the Crane Gallery, including several by Alan Lowndes. He wrote to Andras Kalman with a rather perceptive comment about Alan's paintings. "Alan Lowndes's work is impressive, it will stand a lot of looking at. I don't understand it all, but one is particularly struck by its uncompromising integrity." Few critics could have expressed themselves better.

He set off from Manchester station at midnight with mixed feelings about leaving behind his family, friends and former lover. The train journey took 14 hours, and a tired and somewhat bedraggled Alan Lowndes arrived in St. Ives. Fortunately the summer was a good one. He walked from the station to Fore Street and down the Digey to Back Road and dumped his rucksack by the Porthmeor Studios and walked on; he saw a sign 'St. Peter's Loft', which rang a bell. He walked up the steps and by chance met Bill Redgrave. They talked for a while, then Bill took him round to his home in Island Square; where he met his wife, Mary, called Boots by everyone for reasons he never discovered. Boots very kindly offered him a bed for the night, where he stayed on and off for some time. All the time he was there, "Sundry odd people drifted in and out of the house." Boots and Bill Redgrave were the focal point for many young people living in St. Ives.

He became a porter at the St. Ives Bay Hotel with living accommodation included. In a letter to Kalman he described his job in strong terms. "Myself and a Cornish cretin are engaged in what is glibly termed 'Kitchen Porters' but is really bonded slavery from seven thirty A.M. to 9 P.M. with two and a half hour break in the afternoon during which I sleep or write letters . . . After two weeks here I have seen enough of the place to like it. Despite all the arty crafty pseudo top dressing, the place will be good to paint. Amongst the resident painters, apart from King Ben and Queen Barbara, there seem to be one or two that are quite something."

He soon left this job and found lodgings where he had to share a room with an old crabby Cornish couple. He thought the Cornish came in two types, Boozers and Chapel, the couple were Chapel. On one of his free afternoons, he gained a position as washer up in Pat's Kitchen and some digs in Teetotal Street. He had two interesting colleagues as fellow dish washers, Helga Berlin, the former wife of Sven Berlin, who had left St. Ives by then, and Sylvia. Half way through the season, he took advantage of an offer of a cheaper room at Sylvia's. She had lived in St. Ives for years and was a Salvationist. Her house was on the Stennack, the traditional area for miners as it led out of town and ran alongside the Stennack river. The fishermen lived in Downalong near the harbour, but were being driven out by the artists. Property prices are interesting at that time; it was possible to buy a cottage for £1000.00 in St. Ives and about £100.00 in the country. All the time Alan was taking little breaks to make drawings around the harbour and beaches. On one occasion he attracted a huge crowd watching him paint. He smoked marijuana for the first time in England.

Gradually Sylvia started to mother Alan, which he liked, though was a little concerned by the nods and winks at the café. At the end of the season there was a staff party, and even Pat of Pat's Kitchen was there. He found her a grotesque woman, who in her youth had been accustomed to frequent the Café Royal in its heyday with her mother as chaperone. That evening Alan experienced a serious event that haunted him for days. He had become more than somewhat drunk and had the problem of finding his way back. Somehow his homing instinct took over and off he went up the hill and down past the cemetery. He saw an inviting grass bank and passed out on it. In the morning he was woken up by a light drizzle and didn't know how he had arrived there. He was very alarmed by a grey black angel hovering above him and smaller angels, crosses and gravestones surrounding him. He thought his end had come and leapt up, scrambled over a 10 foot wall and ran home barefooted. He considered this to be the most alarming experience that happened to him in St. Ives. There were others to come in later years.

Alan wrote a letter to Andras Kalman in which he appeared relatively affluent for one of the few times in his life. He might well have become quite a dandy with greater financial resources

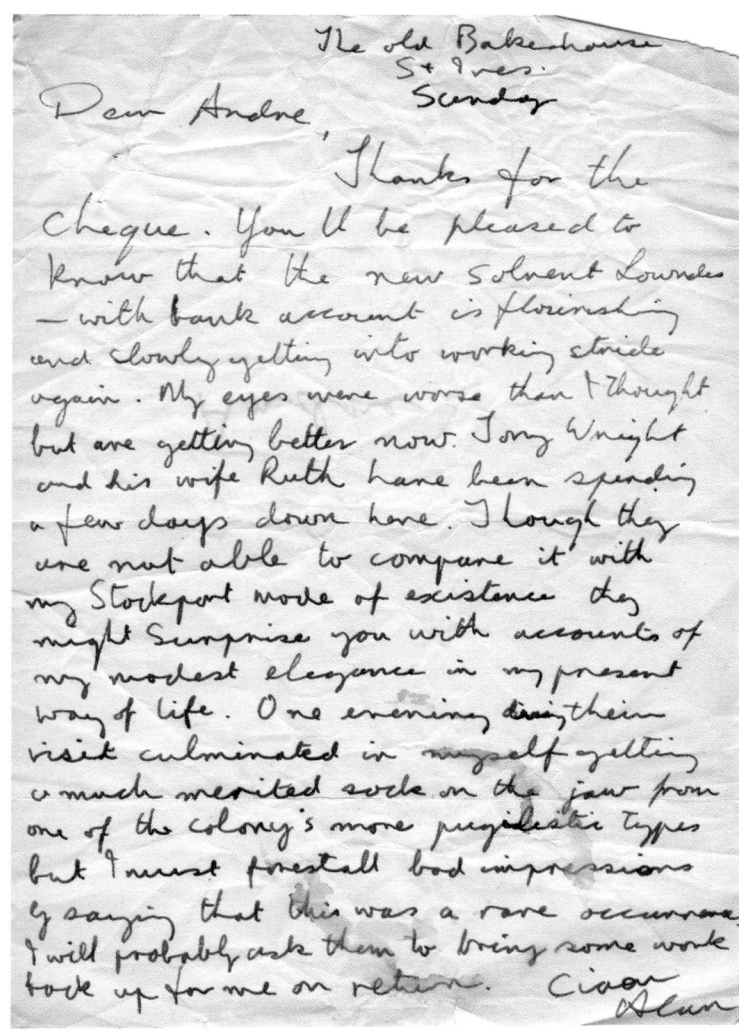

Letter from Alan Lowndes to Andras Kalman in 1955 not long after arriving in St. Ives. It is interesting to note he was involved in fisticuffs at this early stage of his stay in St. Ives.

He wrote to Andras in the autumn of 1955 . . . the weather is getting colder - not as cold yet as elsewhere, no snow or anything but cold enough. Luckily I have a nice warm room to work in and though somewhat lonely at times for - preferably feminine company and one specific person (unattainable - alas!) in particular - things could be worse." Absence and the loss of Cilli still aroused very strong feelings. Kalman had further conversations with Alan where he suggested Alan was not working seriously now but simply 'bumming' around St. Ives. Alan wrote to him from his digs at 9 Teetotal Street ". . . Well I haven't bummed in St. Ives and have had a job ever since I got back. It is now 2.30 a.m. and I am just back from my evening shift, dish washing. From the same conversation I gathered that you don't think much of my painting nowadays. So the news that I am able, with this job, to spend more time at it might mean a lot." He continued with a somewhat self pitying plea to ask whether Kalman wanted to keep him as an artist or not, but "tell me outright." Somehow Lowndes and Kalman always settled their differences; they were still surprisingly close, and Alan had the good sense to appreciate Kalman was speaking objectively and helpfully.

During his withdrawal from social life after his rejection by Cilli, Lowndes claimed, "Amongst the art colony (which was strong then) I was 'the hard to get' of all time, so amongst the girls I couldn't go wrong. I all but had to nail the door up in order to get any work done."[19] He never used this excuse to Andras Kalman to explain his lack of work.

There was always an element of friction between the artist colony and the locals. Both parties could drink prodigiously, but there was also a hint of sexual jealousy. Alan quoted the example of a tall attractive blond girl he had known in Manchester, where she had a nun like reputation. Yet when he brought her back early from a party to avoid her seeing some of the likely excesses, she clung to him and kissed him good night so hard, that he thought she might come right through his shoulder blade. The artists were all into existentialism and tended to wear black - black tee shirt and black jeans. In July he proposed marriage to Jennifer. "She's sweet and twenty (has to have her father's consent) but this is it! Her home is in Richmond, so I'll have to be presented to the family there in the near future." Obviously something went wrong. Jennifer disappears from his scene very quickly.

There were just as strong divisions between groups of artists as there were between artists and locals. The constructivists were deadly rivals of the constructionalists. Anyone who wasn't one or the other was an easel painter and therefore should be banned from the Penwith Art Society. Feelings ran high. ". . . several of the have not painters were refused a bath by their wealthier friends. Even Barbara Hepworth was included amongst the easel painters. Ever since Piet Mondrian had mumbled something about Art towards Architecture, a lot of half baked architects tried painting and sculpture. The Renaissance was cited - but I had always thought it was the other way round, a number of artists had done a bit of architecting." Ben Nicholson was even asked to recant in public and confess the error of his ways by an architect turned artist and another turned critic. Alan resigned from the Penwith Society the same year as Ben Nicholson. At least art was arousing deep and genuine passions.

Later in 1955 he managed to gain free accommodation at Patrick Heron's house, The Eagle's Nest at Zennor in its existing somewhat dilapidated state on condition he helped with the improvement works that were required, especially decorating. The name of the house was very apt, and life must have been somewhat harsh without the usual amenities in such an isolated place. Nevertheless he painted some good pictures there including 'The Eagles' Nest'. He wrote, "The landscape around here is wonderful on a sunny day, colours which I am sure can be seen nowhere else in England nearly stupefy me. When I moved here I began to revise and destroy a lot of the things I had managed to do in St. Ives as I was not happy about them anyway. The trouble here is working in a large studio without heat … Most of the things I am doing now are on hard-board owing to canvas costs." On November 4th and 5th he alleged he did some rather silly things. When he walked into the pub in Zennor, someone managed to insert a firework up his sleeve, or that is his allegation: he of course suffered quite severe burns. He also went midnight bathing. "Nude swimming in November I found has a minimum of sex or romance about it." He happened to lose his wallet when dressing as well as his 'tough' girl and generally was not too pleased.[20]

19 Letter written by Alan Lowndes to Elizabeth Boston (Horsfield/Cilli), 27th September, 1977
20 He complained in several letters to Kalman that the girls were tough in Cornwall

'THE EAGLE'S NEST', 17 x 22.5 inches, Oil on Board, 1955, subtitled 'WHERE NO VULTURES FLY'. Patrick Heron moved into the house in 1956 and remained there until his death in 1999. Many famous men visited this house, including George Mallory of Everest fame and Haile Selassie, Emperor of Ethiopia.

He stayed there until the Spring. On November 15th, 1955 he received a letter from Kalman stating he was not going to continue his endless sentence by sentence debate on their last car journey, it was too tedious. He added that he was going to put on a show of "… your best paintings painted between 1950 and 1955. The title of the exhibition would be: 'Alan Lowndes - A Selection of Paintings 1950-1955'. John Willett has already written an introduction, which I like a lot, and I am hoping to make the catalogue contain six or eight reproductions. The exhibition should open some time towards the middle of January, in competition with the Van Gogh exhibition at the City Art Gallery." He then urged Alan not to be disappointed if not many paintings were for sale. "My intentions are to make this Exhibition a very strong one and give the people a chance to see the best examples of paintings you have done to the present day."[21]

[21] The exhibition was actually titled 'Paintings by Alan Lowndes' at the Crane Gallery Manchester, 14 February – 9 March, 1956. Kalman exhibited 26 paintings, many of them borrowed from various owners, including Daniel Nahum and Mai Zetterling

RIGHT:
'STREET CORNER',
20 x 16 inches, Oil
on Canvas, 1950
Number 2 in the
Catalogue
(Collection of the
Crane Kalman
Gallery)

Two pages from the 1956 catalogue including Alan's first images from Cornwall all dated 1955 and a portrait of Frieda Clowes. Several of the paintings already illustrated in the book were included in the exhibition - Back Alley Girl, Sylvan Grove, Bath Night (Wash Night), Guinness Girl, Self Portrait, Girl in Green, Ice Cream Man, Gas Works, The Harbour, St. Ives.

Pages 82-88 - Early Cornish Subjects

PAGE LEFT (82): 'THE QUAY'. 24 x 18 inches, Oil on Canvas, 1957 (Collection of the Crane Kalman Gallery)

ABOVE: DETAIL OF 'THE HARBOUR'. 22 x 32 inches, Oil on Board, 1956

PAGES OVER (84-85): 'THE ACCORDION PLAYER'. 20 x 29 inches, Oil on Board, 1958, (Private Collection)

Detail of 'Fishing Boats off Smeaton's Pier', *12 x 16 inches, Oil on Board, 1958*
(Collection of the Artist)

'LOGAN ROCK, ROSEWALL HILL'. *16 x 20 inches, Oil on Board, 1967 (Collection of the Crane Kalman Gallery) This is a pleasantly amusing painting with a lovely juxta positioning of the goats and weird shaped rocks. It is somewhat out of chronological order, but is worth including for its humour.*

87

LEFT: 'MAN IN BOAT', *10 x 9 inches, Gouache, 1956 (Collection of Ron Thomas) Alan's method of using gouache as a medium is very similar to his oil paintings, hence many gouaches have been wrongly catalogued as oils.*

At the end of his first year in St. Ives, Lowndes met the Scottish poet Sydney Graham, who was to become his éminence grise. Alan's love of poetry had developed long before he met Sydney. On their first meeting they talked and boozed for about three days and nights round the clock, a harbinger of sessions to come. Sydney had come to St. Ives from Wiltshire, but was no first time visitor, being quite well established there. Like all the others, he was dismayed to find Alan painting 'Old hat representational work'. After a few days of eloquence, Alan tried his hand at 'Picassoid abstracts'; Sydney was a great friend of the painters Robert Colquhoun and Robert MacBryde, who "were doing a Picasso through Yankel Adler at the time." Alan soon realised abstraction was an aberration for him, though poetic expression remained a central core for his painting.

He wrote some interesting comments about Sydney to Kalman, especially their ability to talk as much as each other.

Gradually he became bored with the petty squabbling and ego driven arguments of the artists and went home to Stockport. He spent the next few years alternating between St. Ives and the North, mostly Stockport and Manchester. As ever with Alan, it did not take him long to have serious quarrels with those around him; this double life suited him well.

Chapter 6 - Stockport, Portraits, The Circus, Lowry

Alan stated unequivocally that Stockport always made him want to paint more than St. Ives. He liked above all to know his subject so well, he could concentrate on the actual process of applying the paint; he knew 'every stick and stone' in Stockport. Alan mostly painted earthy moody street scenes, mills and Northerners going about their daily business or enjoying their pleasures in the pub, chip shop, fairs or circus. He painted ordinary people in ordinary situations and became known as the working class painter of working class people. He was never biting or critical, rather affectionate and humorous.

"I always painted the things, people and life around me, bearing in mind that what can be a boring scene, place or person, need not be a boring painting."

He also wrote in 'Why we Paint' whilst discussing his philosophy of painting. "Running through it all is the essential wish to create something which has been defined as soul, essence, spirit, other things. Poetry in a visual sense is the best description I can think of. It is also a partial answer to the big question of why we paint, in that, if we can find out why the poet first began to be a poet, our answer would be on the way. The ancients we are told had an answer to this. Poets had a muse, the goddess, and they worked for her. This is a better answer than saying I work for money or meat. If I could use this answer and be believed, the endless time and trouble it would save.

A lot of my own paintings have been done in Stockport in the grim industrial part of north England. Outside the town is some of the best country landscape in England, the Peak District and the Cheshire Plain. My father who was born in a Cheshire village could never understand why I did not take a trip out to these areas to paint there . . . Painting the slums is not everyone's taste, but it is mine. Sociologically grim as these areas are it was certainly not the political angle which prompted me. I can only repeat that Poetry and attempt to communicate it is the thing that matters. If the attempt is successful, the work achieves a meaning which irrevocably lifts it above the mediocre."

Author and playwright Keith Waterhouse considered Alan's 'working class' paintings doubly important, he was not only painting for the sake of art, but for the sake of history as well. He felt that those who were sociologists in print rather than paint had recently begun to realise that there was such a thing as working class culture in its own right, that displacement of persons need not necessarily mean displacement of personality. Lowndes, instinctively or otherwise, knew this from the very beginning, which is why he did not move.

"It does not take a very shrewd observer to place his work: clearly it belongs somewhere between Arkwright's Spinning Jenny and the Clean Air Act. The tag 'nostalgic' has been hung around Lowndes' neck as often as that one says 'L.S. Lowry' ... those sturdy brick walls the colour of pickled red cabbage, where Lowndes' urchins chalk up their goalposts and wickets must all come tumbling down. Stockport Viaduct itself, unless it has become an ancient monument, will no doubt make way for a spaghetti junction in time. Only the cooling towers will remain. Nostalgia? If it is possible to celebrate a time when people in a certain wage group possessed and were allowed to possess their own sense of order, expressed and were allowed to express their own individuality, formulated and were allowed to formulate the rules of their own society, the charge sticks."[22]

Interestingly, Sir Victor Blank, then the Chairman of G.U.S. (Great Universal Stores) in an interview with a reporter from the Daily Telegraph on January 23rd, 2009, pointed to a painting of a Stockport Street Scene by Alan Lowndes hanging on the wall behind him in his office and stated, "We should never forget where we come from."

Other subject matters also attracted Lowndes. He had completed several portraits of himself, his friends and models. Andras Kalman had been very impressed by a sensitive self-portrait in his first exhibition. Alan's portraits have been hugely underestimated.

22 Keith Waterhouse

PAGE OVER LEFT (90): 'SELF PORTRAIT', 28 x 20.5 inches, Oil on Canvas, 1964 (Collection of the Artist)
PAGE OVER RIGHT (91): DETAIL OF 'PORTRAIT OF JANET, STOCKPORT', also listed as 'Girl in Green', 30 x 20 inches, Oil on Canvas, 1953 (Private Collection)

He had painted his first nude when in art school in Florence in 1946, and said it was all too easy to persuade women to take off their clothes. "For the last hundred years a large part of the painter's training has consisted of drawing and painting the nude. It is not a case of familiarity breeding contempt. In this age of alleged sexual enlightenment, the artist is among the minority not struck by embarrassment or consternation when confronted by a naked human being. Our usual reaction is plain and simple pleasure. A well-painted nude should be erotic in a degree. I will not deny it should be other things as well, but it should definitely be erotic. Whether the female form is our ultimate inspiration of beauty is debateable … I think other things can inspire equal reactions, but a sunset for example cannot be made love to." He had a point.

LEFT PAGE (92) 'CAROLE, MANCHESTER', 24 x 20 inches, Oil on Canvas, 1954 (Private Collection)

'JANET RECUMBENT, STOCKPORT', 24 x 40 inches, Oil on Board, 1952 (Private Collection)

He had always loved the circus, and was given permission to live with the travelling Belle Vue Circus for a month or so in 1959. He made many drawings and paintings of circus people, animals and performers, and continued to paint these scenes for the rest of his life - see pages 242/243 for examples of some of his circus drawings. Sadly his early circus images were lost in a fire in his storeroom/studio in Manchester, where he now painted and stored his pictures. It is more than likely he accidentally set fire to them himself by dropping a cigarette end on the floor. He smoked heavily and usually painted with a brush in one hand and a cigarette in the other, without forgetting his copious drinking. Whatever the cause of the fire, he gained considerable publicity for himself and the local Lucy Clayton model agency. He was featured standing next to Maureen Scopes, the principal of the model agency, with headlines in early 1959:

'Artist Alan Lowndes holds his fire-blistered oil painting for attractive next door neighbour, Maureen Scopes to examine.'
'Blaze wrecks paintings'

'Artist Alan Lowndes was groping through piles of debris in his King Street, Manchester studio to-day - salvaging paintings after a mystery blaze. Attractive Miss Maureen Scopes, new principal of the Lucy Clayton Model Agency, which is next door, discovered the fire after she heard crackling. Smoking nervously, Alan aged 38 said, "I think four pictures have gone, but there may be more." This was not to be the only time fire threatened to burn his paintings and possessions.

Only Alan would have had the good luck to have such an attractive neighbour. He also had the good fortune to be offered temporary studio accommodation in a pub nearly opposite the Granada Studios, which was much frequented by Granada staff. The Landlord, Arthur Gosling, liked art and hung paintings around the wall, several of which were by Alan Lowndes enabling his work to be seen by the journalists and producers at Granada, some of whom like Sir Michael Parkinson bought his work.

LEFT: 'FAIRGROUND GIRL', 20 x 18 inches, Oil on Canvas, 1966

'CLOWNS BOXING MATCH'. *30 x 36 inches, Oil on Canvas, 1974*

'Three Musical Clowns', 28 x 32 inches, Oil on Board, 1960 (Collection of the Artist)

Page Right (97): Detail of 'Three Practising Equilibrists', 30 x 24 inches, Oil on Board, 1964

Lowndes had already achieved fame for murals he painted in the County Hotel in Stockport in 1953. He was always short of money and wanted cash for drinks. The landlord, Bill Goodman employed Alan for part time jobs at the hotel. He heard that Bill wanted to make an upstairs room into a cocktail bar and offered to decorate the room with murals. He suggested they should portray Parisian scenes. Bill Goodman put his foot down on that idea, he did not want any nudes in a family room. Eventually they agreed on a carousel and other fairground features. There is a dispute about what he was paid for his work, and whether some of his reward was in liquid kind. Whatever he received, it was not much. Bill provided the paint, and Alan the labour. Ron Thomas viewed the murals after he had finished. "They were enormous, great big fairground and circus scenes all over the walls in thick paint. The paint alone must have cost a lot of money. He even painted over the fuse-box."

Some years later Alan stated that he undertook the project to gain experience, not to have free beer: it was "a big chance to do a big work. It was very rare for an artist to have a chance to do big work. This was the best opportunity I had in my life to work on a big surface. Every painter wants to paint murals on a wall. No one can take them away." Mrs. Dorothy Goodman, Bill Goodman's wife, described Alan Lowndes as he was at the time of the painting in an article in The Messenger, 13th of July, 1984. "Alan often used to come into the County. He lived in squalor in an attic room in Bamford House higher up Hillgate (Stockport). He was devoted to his painting, nothing else mattered to him. I think he used to come in for the company more than for the drink. One drink would last him all night. He wouldn't spend it on that when he needed it for paints and canvasses. He was terribly thin and nearly always wore sandals. He didn't look as if he ever ate a proper meal. He'd just stand around and chat to anyone who cared for a chat."

About nine years after the completion of the murals, the new landlord, Arthur Drayson, wanted to redecorate the room and paper over the murals. Fortunately his decorator was delayed by other work. In the interval there was sufficient press coverage about Alan's murals to earn them a reprieve. Arthur Drayson changed his plans, when another artist, Derek Guthrie, told him how valuable they were. He became so anxious to preserve them, that he banned the works' table tennis team from practising in the room. Local press and T.V. covered the story. The owner of the local garage, George Warburton explained to the press that the artist had a studio almost across the road from the hotel. He was always hard up. He reckoned that the whole project took Alan about a fortnight to complete, after which he held an exhibition of his paintings in the hotel, mostly Stockport scenes. He then told the tale of Alan's beard, which of course attracted the headlines:

"Shave off beard before you get paid, pub artist told"

George continued, '... when Lowndes asked for his fee, Bill Goodman, the landlord, told him he would have to shave his beard off before he paid him.'

The murals were also featured in the television programme, People and Places. Interviewer Dick Fontaine went to the County Hotel in September 1962 to elicit the opinions of the locals, which were totally predictable: "Customers not impressed by murals". "Alan came in here quite a lot in those days and did the paintings for a few pints of beer and a few shillings in his pocket. Quite honestly that is all I think it's worth." Or, "It has no life and no atmosphere. It is not worth the fuss." Another said, "It is the sort of picture one would expect from a child, certainly not from a practising artist." Such was his appeal to the common man at the time.

Dorothy Goodman held very different views as expressed in the article in the Messenger on 13th of July 1984. "When it was finished the mural was breathtaking. We never had any trouble letting the room. People and coach parties used to come from miles around just to see it, because they had heard about it. They'd ask, 'Who painted it?' When we said Alan Lowndes, they'd say, 'Never heard of him.'" Sadly a few years later the local council demolished the whole hotel in an act of local government indifference to the past in the hope of improvement for the future. There were some attempts to save the hotel, but to no avail. Alas the giant supermarket chain Asda now occupies the site.

Right: Arthur Drayson Landlord of the County Hotel, Stockport, viewing Alan's murals.

The photograph above and the following three photographs by courtesy of Diane Lovelock. They were taken by her husband, Jim Lovelock, who was leading a campaign in 1984 to save the County Hotel and Alan's murals from local council barbarism. Many years earlier, Jim Lovelock used to inhabit part of Bamford House in the market place in Stockport used by Lowndes as his studio.

The Demolition of the County Hotel as permitted by Stockport District Council, July 1984

Jim Lovelock wrote to Andras Kalman requesting assistance to fight the local council. ". . . You may never have known that Alan's biggest was a superb fresco round the walls of the entertainment room at the old County Hotel, where Alan and I used to booze together and where I also played drums in a small jazz outfit. When I returned from one of my mountaineering expeditions I was horrified to find that the pub was being demolished to make way for a supermarket. I tried to get legal restraint on Stockport Council to stop this vandalism of a great work by one of the town's greatest sons."

Andras Kalman replied to Jim Lovelock - ". . . As to Art, they'll remain morons and with today's "quality" newspapers and T.V. going downwards - they will remain for the forseeable future."

GOING, GOING, GONE

Alan suffered comparisons with Lowry all his life. He felt it was 'all too easy for critics to use labels as part of their pet theories'. The usual comments were that Lowndes was a poor man's Lowry; or that Lowry painted sad scenes, whereas Lowndes's subjects were more amusing and human; Lowry was the lonely painter, Lowndes was more sociable: "His (Lowndes) essential spirit is as convivial as Lowry's is lonely.' (John Berger) Or as Andras Kalman, friend of both of them commented, "Lowry would never have painted the busts and bums seen in such ample proportions in Lowndes's work." Ian Gale, one of the subtlest and most observant critics of Lowndes's work, considered that "Lowndes's vividly concocted human situations are entirely different from Lowry's pictures . . . which are rather records of incidents." John Willett felt that "Lowndes saw himself as a follower of Lowry, and if his apparent naivety was not quite so sly, he viewed his rather similar subjects with a comparable sense of the incongruous." Alan would certainly have agreed with Sir Michael Parkinson's comment, "Who's to say what's good or bad? Our appreciation is as good as anybody's. There's a lot of intellectual crap written about art."

Alan Lowndes always denied there were even any comparisons with Lowry in his style of painting, he just painted the same type of scenes in the same area of the country. As he said, "I began to paint the local scene before I had seen a Lowry. At first, when I saw one, I really didn't like his work; it was very much in opposition to mine. The only thing we have in common is the subject, the mills, the streets, and all that is available to everybody. Our approaches are quite different." Above all, a close look at a painting by Lowry will show all his figures captured in a moment of time, motionless, whereas Lowndes's figures are clearly drinking, moving or loafing and very much alive. Like Lowry, he was the only painter working full time at painting, though he considered Lowry to be in a better position than he, because he was making a good living by then. Above all, where are human emotions in a Lowry painting, which are so prevalent throughout Lowndes's work?

"I readily accept there is a common theme running through our work, but there is a notable difference, which is this:- Lowry comes from a middle class background. His father was in the estate agency business. Lowry also had a small unearned income. He went to the industrial community in Salford and painted it as an outside observer. This isn't the case with me. I grew up in the working class I painted. I observed it from the inside." Lowry was the observer from without. Lowndes was painting from within. Alan gave an example of the way critics use labels. "When Lowry moved out to Mottram, he began painting a bit of Derbyshire. He can paint a green field using for the most part a whiteish sort of grey and convince you it's a green field. It's not snow. This is where critics compare him to Breughel. Only because he's got a whiteish-grey affair and Breughel painted a lot of scenes on ice ... they snatch at straws." Alan must have been more than somewhat annoyed by so many comparisons with Lowry's style. He didn't resemble Lowry in the way he applied his paint nor in his brushwork, though both painters certainly shared common views about arrogant critics.

Perhaps the words of Terrance Mullaly in the Daily Telegraph, December 13th, 1972 sum up Lowndes better than most.

"Lowndes looks at the world directly. He has no use for conventions, either academic or the avant garde. What he does have is a considerable feeling for oil paint. At the same time and most important, he is a witty observer. Above all Alan Lowndes makes the ordinary seem terribly important."

Alan soon came to know Lowry and admired him as a man and artist. Critics and writers seldom mention the amount of support that Lowry gave all his fellow artists. He always attended their openings and gave them much encouragement. The artist William Turner reveres Lowry for what he did for him. Nicholas Horsfield was most impressed by Lowry's skill in making one feel special with very personal words of encouragement, but was a little surprised when he heard him use very similar expressions for someone else. He was more politically astute than one has been led to believe. Sam Junior told the story that Alan lived with Lowry for a few weeks, when he had moved to Mottram. It is impossible to verify the story, but there is no doubt that Sam was convinced of its veracity.

Alan took Sam Junior and Slim Ingram to tea with Lowry in Mottram. "He was a fantastic little man, very enthusiastic and outgoing all the time. He made us more than welcome. After that, I was manager of a theatre and I booked in the Northern Ballet. They did a production of Matchstick Men. Sadly the artistic director played Lowry. I went up to him after the performance and said, "Lowry wasn't an idiot." He played him like he was mentally handicapped."[23] Ron Thomas tells of the occasion Alan asked Tom Hassell to meet Lowry. The two of them duly arrived at his front door. Alan knocked and the door opened. Alan asked Lowry if they could come in, a close friend wanted to meet him. The response surprised them. "You (Alan) can come in, you (Tom) can't." No doubt he was tired of people calling on him as his fame was growing.

Later in February 1976 when L.S. Lowry died, Michael McNay of the Guardian rang a few of Lowry's friends, including Andras Kalman and Alan Lowndes, asking them to write a short appreciation. These appeared in the Guardian the next day. Alan's piece concluded:

"Northern people don't go much for eulogies, but I think he should be buried in Westminster Abbey. He will be remembered when a lot of the soup tins of today are forgotten. Once I went round a show of chimpanzee paintings with him. We did not say much. At the end he said: 'Well, they have a good sense of balance, but they have to.' Rob Wilton could not have put it better."

Today, comparisons are not made between Lowndes and Lowry, partly because it is easier to see why the two artists are so different, and partly because several other northern artists have come to the fore - Arthur Delaney (1927 - 1987), Theodore Major (1908 - 1999) and William Turner (b. 1920), to name a few, who appear far closer to Lowry than Lowndes. Or as Matisse commented, "Whether we like it or not, we belong to our time and we share its opinions, its feelings, even its delusions."

23 Slim Ingram

'Washing Day'. 32 x 25 inches. Oil on Board. 1958

'ICE CREAM MAN', 54 x 77 inches, Oil on Board, 1956 (This painting has gained another title, 'THE ICE CREAM SELLER', which was added later. In the Crane Kalman exhibition of 1961-62 it was titled Ice Cream Man.)

'DANCING GIRLS'. 20 x 15.5 inches, Gouache on Card, 1958 (Collection of Betty Goldfield)
This painting is another example of a gouache that looks very like an oil and has been catalogued as such.

'Rosemary Street, Stockport', *24 x 32 inches, Oil on Canvas, 1958*

'CAT BEWILDERED'. *18 x 16.5 inches, Gouache, 1958*

'HIGH STREET, STOCKPORT', *24 x 29 inches, Oil on Board, 1959 (Collection of Bill Clark)*

Chapter 7 - John and Anne Willett, Valerie, Marriage and Honeymoon in Normandy

JOHN WILLETT

Alan had formed a close friendship with John Willett and his wife Anne. John had joined the Guardian as Chief Foreign Leader Writer in the days when it was the Manchester Guardian and he lived with Anne in a flat in Salford. "We never saw our view, we had a view, but the air was never clear until there had been a Bank Holiday. John had started writing the odd article about the art scene in Manchester. He came to know Andras Kalman, whom he found to be a most congenial companion. Only the second time we were in the gallery, there was this young man with a memorable face and sort of frizzy wild hair, Alan Lowndes, with a stammer that was absolutely unforgettable. He seemed to have learned a strange way of making it worth waiting for the ending. The key word of everything he was saying was at the end."[24]

An incident occurred that was an augury of Alan's life ahead. The Willetts' only vehicle was a van they had bought cheaply from a friend. They decided to take Alan out to a pub they liked in Manchester, and an awful lot was tippled. In the general conversation and banter, the Willetts had not noticed how much Alan had absorbed. Whilst driving home from the pub, there was no movement in the back. On arrival, Anne Willett opened the back door and found Alan passed out completely unconscious in the position of the crucifix; they had very great difficulty getting him out. Unfortunately Alan was in the habit of drinking copiously without eating: sadly this habit was to attack his already fragile liver more quickly than it might have done.

Not long after this visit to the pub, John and Anne were enjoying a picnic by a canal near Manchester and discussing whether they should stay in the area or not. They noticed that the foam on the water was orange, red and yellow; they left. John wanted to be independent to write books on art and politics and translate Brecht. They drew circles round London, which became ever wider, but in the end decided to buy a property in Normandy, a lovely house nine miles from Dieppe at a price considerably less than a cottage in England. The man who had built the house and designed the lovely garden had been executed during the Revolution.

---

24 Anne Willett, who had been brought up in France and spoke French fluently. It must have been quite a shock for her to have to live in the filthy air of Salford at that time.

They tried to keep in touch with Alan on the telephone. "It took a long time to hear what he had to say."[25] so they invited him to stay with them in Normandy in the summer of 1956. They thought he would be receptive to the area because of the subject matter of his pictures, and it had always been a favourite area for artists from the time of Courbet onwards. Anne Willett added, "These artists came to Normandy because of the light, but also the sea air protected their eyes from getting sore and tired. People like Monet and that were aware of it. You don't need any salt for the lamb, because the animals breathe in all the salt air. Sickert lived there and had three homes, he was very discreet to whom he gave the right address."

They were expecting Alan, but he couldn't say exactly when he would arrive, as he was coming by bicycle all the way from Manchester. Not surprisingly it took him a long time to reach Newhaven and then across the channel to Dieppe. Anne became very concerned one day, when she noticed a body in the hedge opposite. It had probably been run over and the person had just thrown it there. "The legs were sticking out, it was horrible." She asked her husband to phone the police, while she went to see if there was anything that could be done. It took her several minutes to recognise it was Alan Lowndes. Alan had been involved in a fracas in Newhaven, where he had lost his money and his bicycle and had to walk to the ferry and then all the way to their house after landing. He was exhausted, but also too embarrassed to enter this rather grand house or to explain the reality of what had happened to him.

He stayed for a long time and painted quite a few pictures. Alan mixed well with the many distinguished people that stayed that summer. He used his stammer to make some witty comments that endeared him to all. Once he was asked whether he knew Barbara Hepworth. He replied. "YYYYYYes." 'What is she like?' "Ssssssssssometimes her gggggggranite features ssssssssoften into a sssssssteely glare." On a trip to Paris with the Willetts, Alan toyed with the idea of living in the city for a year. He told Andras that Anne Willett had shown him how cheap the rents were, which could even be afforded by him. In the end he decided Paris was not for him, he preferred St. Ives and Manchester.

In Stockport a very different tale was emerging. Alan of course had no money for the return ferry. He spun his family a tale that his agent had sold some of his pictures in France, but had not been paid. He had to cycle to France to drag the money from these people, because he could not afford any other way. Unfortunately he had to sell his bicycle to pay his costs getting there and was now without any money, so could they please fund his return journey? They were well used to Alan's pleas for money, but relented and sent him some. Both his brothers, Sam and Colin, regarded him as a scrounger professing the unimportance of money, but always asking for it. To Kalman he produced a different tale explaining the loss of his money in Newhaven. Nevertheless Andras sent him some francs and received grateful thanks.

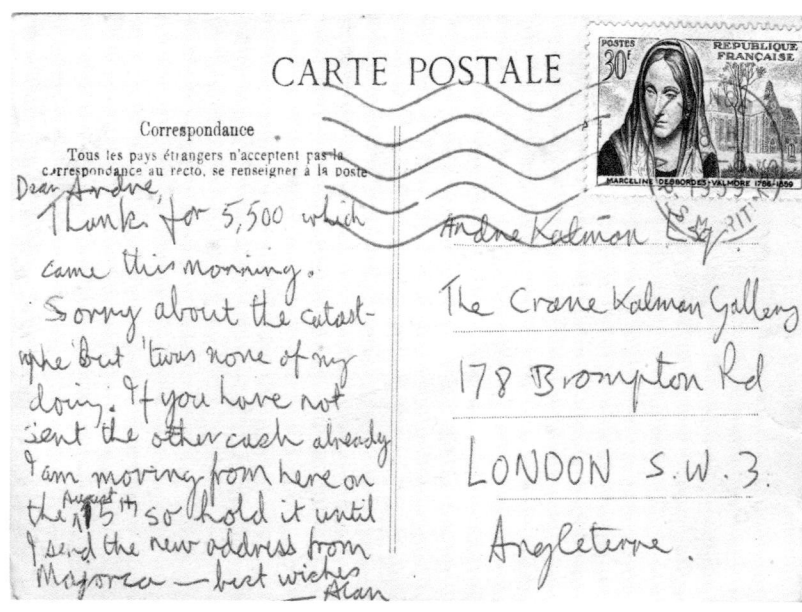

Card from Alan to Andras Kalman thanking him for money sent

[25] Anne Willett.

It was during this visit to the Willetts' house that Alan heard that his father had died. He was totally overcome by the news. One of the great influences of his life had gone forever: he remained profoundly affected by his father's death for many years. Alan had always regarded him as a 'living it up' sort of man. His father had been such an important part of his emotional life, especially remembering his mother had died when he was only three, and now his father too was gone for ever.

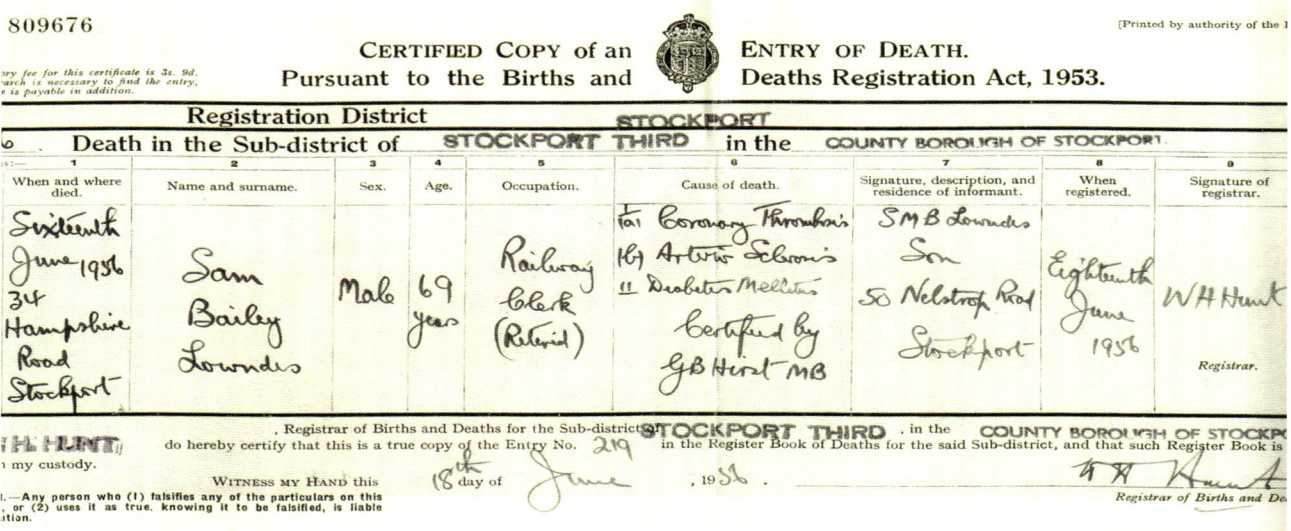

Sam Bailey Lowndes's death certificate, 18th of June, 1956. He died of Coronary Thrombosis, Arterio Sclerosis and Diabetes Melitus.

After his times in Cornwall and Dieppe, he returned in 1958 to Manchester on one of his northern visits, a trip that was not altogether happy. He was constantly ill and had terrible problems with his teeth, many of which were extracted. He quarrelled with Pauline and Reg, Kalman's employees at the Crane Gallery, who were looking after the gallery at the time.[26] He considered Pauline officious and petty and Reg as 'stupid, capable of being no more than an odd job man'. Both he and Ron Thomas felt the gallery was being run very badly in Kalman's absence. Reg and Pauline made him feel rather unenthusiastic about his future exhibition: he had noticed the absence of sales in the previous two exhibitions. There was also a huge argument about Alan abusing his position at the gallery by staying overnight and inviting friends to accompany him. In a letter to Kalman he tried to point out he worked at night, and they only talked until the morning, because none of them had anywhere else to go. As ever he made a strong plea for some money.

Somehow, whether through the influence of Andras Kalman, John Berger or John Willett and Nicholas Horsfield, Alan managed to obtain a place at the Karolyi foundation in Vence, southern France in 1959. The foundation had been set up by Count Karolyi to further international understanding between artists and writers. Unfortunately the Count had died and left his wife, the Countess, with very little money. Ron Thomas knew Alan was going there and offered to give him a lift. The offer was declined, but they agreed to meet there. Ron was working in Holland at the time: he and a Dutch friend drove down to Vence to meet him. Lowndes was living in a small bungalow designed for two people at the bottom of the garden with a lovely purpose built artist's studio attached.

26 Kalman was setting up his new gallery in Knightsbridge, the Crane Kalman Gallery

His companion in the bungalow was the American writer, Stetson Kennedy. The third member of the group staying at the house was a young woman from Sheffield, Valerie Holmes. She had been employed by the Countess as a typist and secretary to assist her in completing her book. Valerie had previously spent five years working in Paris and spoke French fluently. Countess Karolyi had come from one of the wealthiest families in Europe and had known the emperor, Franz Joseph. She used to ask Valerie to run many errands for her and to visit the 'artists' to ensure they were working. Last of all was Georges, the gardener, but would-be artist. He was tall and remarkably good-looking. "the most handsome man I have ever met." (Valerie Lowndes) Ron Thomas joined the general group for a day or two and reported that Alan was in pursuit of an American girl, who did not want to know him. One day he took Alan and Valerie to the beach, and "Alan certainly noticed Valerie when she put on her bikini."

'To Valerie with Love, Alan', 22.5 x 14.5 inches, Oil on Board, 1959 (Collection of the Artist)

RIGHT: 'THE STUDIO, VENCE, ALPES MARITIME', 18 x 24 inches, Oil on Board, 1959. This building was Alan's shared studio at the Karolyi Foundation

The summer was the hottest on record for the century. The small group at the foundation socialised together and became very close and intense in the great heat. Soon Alan and Valerie were 'going together', especially when Valerie left the countess to live in the town. There was much talk of fire that hot summer. One day Valerie and Stetson were having a cup of coffee in the square and saw the fire engine tearing up. They were horrified to see it heading for the Foundation.

There are two versions to account for what occurred. Alan had seen the fire approaching and had told the countess to fetch her car and leave; she refused. He suggested that she should remove her valuables; she claimed she had none. He took his paintings out of the house and moved them away as far as he could. The situation was becoming all too familiar with the fire in his Manchester studio. The fire reached his bungalow and burnt what few clothes he had, but the pictures were saved. In another version, it is just as likely Alan set fire to his chalet himself. He constantly smoked, drank and was very careless, as was seen in his Manchester studio fire. By the time Stetson and Valerie reached the foundation, Alan had consumed a bottle of whisky and was very drunk. The Countess was naturally not at all amused, and Valerie had to calm ruffled feathers.

His dealer, Andras Kalman was not too impressed with most of his work in Vence; as he said, "He painted unsuccessful pictures. The boules playing Frenchmen somehow looked just the same as the milkman in Stockport." Kalman had written a letter to Lowndes urging him to be true to himself and not be diverted by 'the smart designers of St. Ives'. He wrote again on November 29th, 1959. "Don't try to be a canary. By that I mean that to most discriminating people the pictures of yours that give the most satisfaction are those done in the north of England . . . Lowry has been very, very strong and intelligent not to try to go and paint abroad, where he might have lost the flavour that gives that strength and integrity to his pictures."

Alan agreed with this opinion of his work in a letter to Kalman dated November 24th, 1959. "The remarks you make about the work that I did abroad this year are sadly enough all too true. Just before your letter arrived I was thinking on the lines you suggested about memory paintings. No more canary stuff!!!"

Valerie decided it was time to go home to Sheffield. Alan and Stetson went to Ibiza, then an unknown unspoilt small island, from which they went to Formentera.[27] Valerie felt lost at home and missed Alan dreadfully. She wrote a letter to Alan care of the Crane Kalman Gallery, which was the address Alan had given her. By some miracle the letter reached him in Formentera, and by "another miracle he wrote back suggesting they should meet in France, because he was on his way to Dieppe to meet the Willetts." They managed to converse by phone and arranged for Valerie to go to Dieppe by ferry, where Alan would meet her. John Willett actually met Valerie and suggested that she and Alan should go to Paris for a while, as their house was full of guests. So Alan and Valerie spent two marvellous weeks in Paris. In the heady atmosphere Alan proposed marriage and Valerie accepted. Alan had raised the subject a few weeks earlier in Vence, but Valerie had considered that far too premature. Alan used to joke that he only married Valerie because she spoke French and he needed her to translate for him.

They arranged a time and date for the wedding service with the British Embassy and a small reception afterwards in the Hotel D'Iena, Paris. Valerie wanted to marry straight away; she thought she might change her mind if she delayed. Mr. and Mrs. Holmes, Anne Willett, the handsome Georges, Stetson Kennedy and his new girlfriend Paula and Andras Kalman were to be the guests, as well as some of Valerie's friends and colleagues in Paris, but none of Alan's family came. Nothing ever seemed simple for Alan. He wrote to Andras Kalman inviting him to attend the wedding on the wrong date, later corrected in another letter; it was not his fault, the embassy had changed the date for their wedding. He introduced him to his future wife with suitably comforting words.

Later in the letter he states, "As I have only my cord slacks and sports coat plus a couple of shirts remaining as my wardrobe, it would be good if you could bring the suit you mentioned." Kalman brought his suit for Alan to wear at the wedding and reception. Unfortunately the plane was delayed and he could not make the service, causing Alan to attend his wedding ceremony in his minimal outfit. Stetson Kennedy and Paula did not turn up at all. There was nothing that could be done, the service had to be completed with Alan garbed as he was. When they came to the hotel, Andras arrived with the wedding suit,

ABOVE RIGHT: 'ROOFS IN IBIZA', *12 x 8.5 inches, Pencil, 1959*

[27] Alan wrote to Kalman from Formentera, "I just missed eloping with the Countess Karolyi's English secretary a plain homely girl from Sheffield." He was soon to change his opinion about Valerie's looks and personality.

and Alan was at least able to look smart for the reception. An official at the embassy complained to Kalman he had never seen a scruffier groom. Andras, who was never slow to take advantage of any publicity, used a suitably embellished story for the press.

MANCHESTER
EVENING NEWS,
OCTOBER 1959

Wedding day at the British Embassy, Paris, Monday, October 12th, 1959. Alan centre, Georges on his right, Mrs. Holmes on his left. Valerie took the photograph and is therefore not featured.

After the wedding they had been invited to spend their honeymoon at the Willett's house in Le Thil-Manville near Dieppe. Anne had asked Valerie whether she wanted to be alone for a short time, or, would she like them to be there? Valerie asked if they could be alone for a short time. That was fine. Anne had some business in Dieppe. All went well at the reception and the two of them found their way to Le Thil-Manneville for their wedding night.

Anne and John Willett returned to Le Thil with Peter Taylor and his wife Elise after a suitable interval for Alan and Valerie to enjoy their house on their own. Peter, a very 'proper Englishman', was the British Consul in Dieppe. He had lived in Dieppe all his life apart from his spell at an English boarding school. Elise was from one of the more respectable remittance families in Dieppe. That evening Anne cooked them a meal, and afterwards they all went to bed. At about 2 a.m. Anne woke Valerie and Alan to say some friends of theirs were downstairs. Stetson Kennedy, Georges and Paula had turned up. Stetson and Paula claimed that they thought the wedding was at 11 p.m. and they had all lost their way in the village. (An interesting statement, as Georges had attended the wedding) Alan had given them directions saying that the Willett's house was the first in the village. Unfortunately the trio had approached the village from the opposite direction. They became lost and woke up several people to ask the way. A tourist had been shot for doing just that the previous year.

The Willetts' house in Le Thil-Manneville, Normandy

They were all invited to lunch with Baroness Diana de Bosmelet at her chateau in Auffay, but the Willetts wisely thought it was better that they went to lunch with the Baroness, and the Lowndes entourage looked after themselves. The Chateau at Bosmelet was the centre of one of the most important and unknown acts of heroism in World War II. The 17th century Chateau de Bosmelet was situated on the highest point closest to London, an ideal site for the Germans to use as a launch pad for the V1 rockets.

Hitler had planned to fire 5000 rockets a month, but was foiled by the ingenious work of Michel Hollard, who investigated some unusual building sites that had been reported to him by the local branch of the resistance. Posing as a forester, he found the V1 bunkers and painstakingly reported their location to the R.A.F. crossing the border to Switzerland on foot 98 times at considerable risk to his life, let alone his enormous physical and mental challenges, a remarkable feat. The R.A.F. targeted the Chateau de Bosmelet on no less than 28 occasions. The bombing was so successful, that only about 2400 doodlebugs (V1s) in total landed in Britain. In 1994, the small town of Auffay created a tribute to the work of this remarkable man by naming the square in front of the station the Place Michel-Hollard. On April 27th 2004, Michel was further honoured for his work when Eurostar named one of their trains the 'Michel Hollard'.

Michel Hollard received the Croix de Guerre in both world wars, the Médaille de la Résistance, the Légion d'Honneur with rosette, and the D.S.O., the highest British decoration that can be given to a foreigner. It was Lt. General Sir Brian Horrocks who called him "the man who literally saved London" and added, "it seems to me that many statues have been erected in London, the city he saved, to less deserving people."

The Chateau de Bosmelet

After allied bombing (left) and after Diana's extensive restoration at huge personal cost (right).

V1 bunker and launch site, Chateau de Bosmelet, *20th November, 2004*

After a few very sociable days in Le Thil-Manneville, Alan and Valerie left for St. Ives, and the others went to Paris. Meanwhile in Stockport, Alan with his mischievous sense of humour had spread stories that he had married a countess. No doubt he well may have liked to have done, but his friends felt he had bettered himself by marrying Valerie, who came from a middle class home in Sheffield. Nevertheless, even at that stage John Willett told his wife Anne he thought the marriage would last. However he did say to Valerie, "Alan isn't difficult, he is impossible." Alan mischievously commented to Elizabeth Boston, "I had a mixed marriage. I married from Yorkshire."

Alan had written to Andras Kalman that he would now be leading a more settled life, which meant more work done. "I will be glad - only too glad - to settle down & work. This year in which there have been more upsets & travels than usual for me has quite fed me up with unsettled living. Believe it or not to establish myself with some permanency and with the right girl has long been an aim of mine." In many letters between Alan and Andras over the years, shortage of money, lack of work and a settled lifestyle featured constantly.

'TOURETTE SUR LOUPE'. *1959. 19.5 x 19 inches, Oil on canvas. This painting is very important emotionally for Valerie Lowndes. Tourette is near Vence, where her love affair with Alan commenced. (Private Collection)*

Chapter 8 - Cornwall Part 1, 1959 to the mid Sixties, St. Ives, Halestown

Alan had telephoned his friend, the sculptor John Milne, prior to leaving France and asked him if he could find him a flat. During Alan's visits to Cornwall, he had come to know John quite well whilst living with him at different times helping him 'do up' Trewin, the large house Cosmo Roedewald had bought for John. Cosmo, John Milne's benefactor and partner was extremely jealous of Alan's relationship with Milne. He needn't have worried. Alan was entirely heterosexual. Or as he put it to Kalman, "John is a bit precious, but I am still old fashioned and like women."

"By that time it was October, and that summer just lasted and lasted. It was warm and we moved into this little flat, and oh I was so tired, we'd packed up and done the crossing and an overnight train journey, which used to take a good 12 hours from London to St. Ives. We went to the pub (The Sloop) in the evening and everyone was there, but they always were, the pub was full of artists. They were going on to a party at John Milne's. The last thing I wanted to do was to go to a party, because I was dead tired, and I was not dressed up. We went with Sydney and Nessie (Graham), and the party was in honour of Francis Bacon. Bryan Wynter and Monica (Wynter) were there and Terry and Kath (Frost). It was quite a select party - that was my introduction to St. Ives. It was a hectic winter, lots of parties, gatherings, so that is where it all started."[28]

Sydney Graham welcomed Valerie to St. Ives with a poem and cartoon.

St. Ives was a severe culture shock for Alan's new wife. The 'art talk' was like a foreign language, which made her feel just as she did when she first arrived in Paris and could not understand French. "How can I learn art?" She asked Alan. "Just look at paintings." He replied. Eventually she learned a little about art and began to feel a member of the group. The artists of the area used to meet at the 'Artists' Table' in the Sloop. Valerie did not enjoy the long hours spent in the pub. She was used to civilised wine drinking in the French cafes, where no one became drunk, whereas some people in the Sloop seemed determined to become drunk and troublesome.

At first Alan worked in the front room of their little flat, but soon the Lowndes moved to a house in the Digey, Number 18, which they bought with Valerie's savings. They had debated whether to buy out of town or near the centre. The Grahams had urged them to buy in the

BACKGROUND PAINTING - 'PORTRAIT OF JOHN MILNE', 29.75 x 20 inches, Oil on Canvas Board, 1956

28 Valerie Lowndes

country, where it was so much cheaper. Valerie's mother had always advised her to be near the shops. The house was close to many of their friends, the Frosts were just round the corner and Bob Crossley was at the end of the road. "It was a fisherman's cottage with absolutely no ground, you'd leave the front door open onto some steps onto the street, and there was a stable door on the side that one always had to have open, because there was no daylight into the basement kitchen, so everybody could see that you were there and call in or shout out, the house was never your own."

18 THE DIGEY

LEFT: ANTONIA HASSELL AND FELIX THE CAT, 1960s

RIGHT: VALERIE LOWNDES, 2004

Alan and Valerie had already enjoyed dinner on several occasions with John Milne and Boots and Bill Redgrave, now Valerie could return their hospitality. She had lived in Paris for four years and was fully used to giving dinner parties. Their usual guests at this time were John Milne, Boots and Bill Redgrave, Nancy Wynne-Jones, Tony O'Malley and anyone staying in the house. Alan tried very hard to interest Andras Kalman in O'Malley's work. Unfortunately Kalman thought his landscapes were 'sort of Yeats-ish Irish blarney affair - almost touristy.' He could never have foreseen O'Malley's successes years later in Ireland. Though their kitchen was quite dark in the daytime, it looked particularly well in the evening - candle lit and wooden beams on the ceiling. The house may have been small and somewhat public, but it was certainly fertile. The Lowndes had all three of their children in the Digey, Mandy in 1960, Martin in 1962 and Rosalind in 1964.

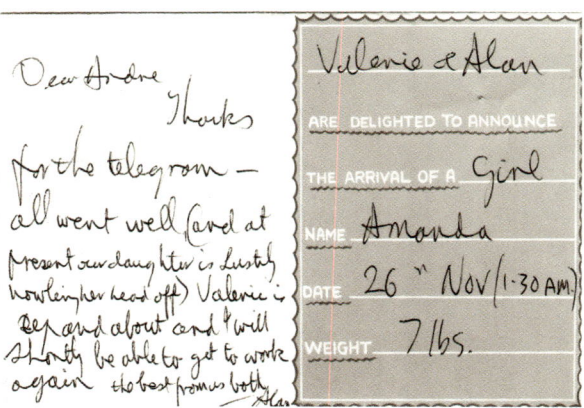

Alan was painting well, inspired by the sea, colour, scenery and ruggedness of Cornwall, but also by the congenial life based around the Sloop.[29] Most of the artists used to gather at the 'artists' table', often 20 at a time to enjoy a convivial lunchtime discussing art with like-minded people, the standard tipple being half a pint of bitter at 7d. Regulars included Tony O'Malley, Peter Lanyon, Patrick Heron, Terry Frost, Karl Weschke, Willie Barnes-Graham, Bryan Wynter, Denis Mitchell, John Milne, Anthony Benjamin, and Roy Conn. Francis Bacon stayed in St. Ives during the winter of 1959 and spent most evenings in the Sloop. He

---

29 Alan's greatest success in 1961 was Kalman's sale of 'Foggy Evening' to Hugh Williams, the author of 'The Grass is Greener' and 'The Irregular Verb to Love' amongst others.

was friendly with everyone. Painting is a lonely solitary existence. Most of the artists used their time at the Sloop in talking, arguing and exchanging ideas and would then return to their tasks, like Terry Frost, who would have one drink and say, "Kathy has got the dinner on the table." Denis Mitchell was the same. There were one or two who had different ideas, especially Sydney Graham, who quickly became Alan's chief drinking companion. They would continue drinking "all afternoon and evening and all the next day and the next, all without food. He seemed to prefer the Sloop to his own home."[30]

RIGHT: 'SYDNEY GRAHAM', 24 x 18 inches, Oil on Board, 1960 (Private Collection)

One evening after the Sloop, Alan and Valerie went to Willie Barnes-Graham's house with Bacon. Brian Wall was living with Willie at the time, and the four of them had a long discussion about European art. "After an hour or two Willie made some cheese on toast, and then we went home. Life was extremely sociable; there were parties every week-end, often given by non-artists. A couple of wealthy divorcees had rented places for the winter and vied with each other to give parties. Out of town artists gave parties, the poorer ones such as Karl Weschke and Michael Heard were bring-your-own-drink affairs; Patrick Heron's and Peter Lanyon's were more formal. Some of the bring your own parties became rowdy and even violent, especially if Sydney Graham turned up."[31]

Sydney Graham was an imposing man physically with a mesmeric voice who dominated all those around him. He and his wife Nessie were given much assistance by Nancy Wynne-Jones, a relatively wealthy woman, who was generous in her support of impecunious artists and writers. Her father had been the Lord Lieutenant of Wales. At this time Sydney had very little money, but there was something special about him, which made people want to look after 'Sydney and Nessie'. Alan found him fascinating, and the respect was mutual. Graham's poetry has been re-appraised in recent times and has gained much respect and approval. Unfortunately for Valerie and the family, Sydney's visits increasingly became dreaded. He would say "Och we are catching the next bus home, my dear and don't worry now, we are just going to sit here and have a wee glass of whisky and then we are away on the two o'clock bus. They never caught the bus and were there all afternoon and evening. Sydney was a big man, his drunken staggering about and falling over in our very small house was rather difficult, especially with our young children."[32]

She was glad of the occasions when Alan and Sydney decided they would go to the Coastguard's Cottage by the Battery on the Island, St. Ives, where Nancy Wynne-Jones lived. They would stay there for two or three days and nights drinking and being 'creative', often with a tape recorder, which was a very new electronic gadget in those days. They took preludin to keep them awake for their lengthy sessions. "They thought they were being very clever enacting whatever they did, but they did realise it was a load of nonsense, when they played it back next morning. So they were perceptive enough to realise that. But it did not stop them, they would go on another three day bender, as they called it."[33] Sometimes Tony O'Malley, a gentle kind Irishman, would drop in when the three were up at the Battery and would comment, "Och, the circus has left toon." Eventually Nancy Wynne-Jones would drive the two of them back, and Alan would collapse in his bed for many hours.

SYDNEY GRAHAM (LEFT) AND TONY O'MALLEY (RIGHT), ST. IVES, 1960s

THE BATTERY AND COASTGUARD'S COTTAGE ON THE ISLAND, ST. IVES, CORNWALL

32 & 33 Valerie Lowndes

"In spite of all this, I became very fond of Sydney and Nessie. I loved to hear him read his poetry and to sing Scottish songs, a favourite being 'My Love is like a Red Red Rose'. Years later when Alan was asked in a Gloucestershire hospital if he'd like something played on the hospital radio, he chose this song. Nessie too had a fund of songs, one she often sang to our children. 'Coulter's Candy', I now sing to my grandchildren."[34]

Sadly no food was usually consumed. These activities would have had a dramatic strain on a fit man's body, on Alan's it was serious. During his northern days, Alan never had enough money to drink much more than beer, but now he had Valerie to assist with some management of their income, whisky and spirits came more to the fore. His drinking bouts with Sydney became notorious in the area. Alan Corker, a close friend from Upper Cam days recalled Alan saying to him that Sydney was the best 'chucker out' in pubs he had ever met. When drunk, Alan could have a sharp tongue and create many an acrimonious situation. Michael Hunt, who manages Boots Redgraves' former gallery, recalls that Alan when drunk was rude and truculent, but great when sober. "He was not as bad as one very famous artist who was impossible when drunk. He used to come into the hotel I was managing and march into the dining room to urinate on the floor in front of my guests to make some sort of point."[35] In her autobiography Nancy Wynne-Jones described Alan as a "truculent little man".

Peter Lanyon used to call on the Lowndes at least four times a year to collect works for the Newlyn Art Gallery. He had a long-standing feud with Barbara Hepworth and the Penwith Gallery, but supported Michael Canney, artist and curator at the Newlyn. He would stay and chat when he called, and also gave the Lowndes a lift to the opening. "He was tall, good-looking, fair, friendly and with a ready laugh. He was liked by many, but not by Barbara, it was a sad day when he died young in a gliding accident." Peter Lanyon died on August 31st, 1964 at Taunton as a result of his injuries suffered in the accident.

There was another side to Alan that was kindly, amusing and entertaining. Jane Mitchell, widow of the sculptor Denis Mitchell recalled one of the parties in Fore Street. A Canadian couple living in St. Just had left their baby on its own to attend the party. Jane was very worried about the baby; Alan was the only person to back her up and show concern. She regarded him as a very kind man. "He was fun, that is all I can say." Alan was not the 'life and soul of a party', but he enjoyed them and was entertaining. He loved telling stories and declamations like 'Albert and the Lion' using his stammer to dramatic effect. "He liked music, he liked dancing, we danced a lot, we both used to like dancing, liked dancing at parties."[36]

The painter, Karl Weschke found Alan to be a man who stuck to his guns, very 'short of stature holding a cigarette.' Karl wasn't sure whether he was 'mad or queer', but later found out he was a real Northerner. "He was very direct, but made me familiar with Lowry. I had much discussion with him about art in general, he was a wholehearted man and painter. I remember saying 'A cow can't help being a cow, a painter can't help being a painter. Some cows are better milkers than others'. I suspected his constant flow of humour was a self-defensive act, hiding behind a quip."[37] He remembered an extraordinary evening he witnessed in the Tinner's Arms at Zennor. He arrived to find three men having a heated argument, Alan Lowndes, Jeremy Le Grice and Conor Fallon. "Unfortunately all three suffered from a serious stammer, so there was a lot of Humf etc., it was hard to keep a straight face."[37]

The Painter Roger Hilton used to visit Alan and Valerie, when he came on his occasional trips to St. Ives from London. She used to wait nervously for his call, having heard of his heavy drinking and aggressive behaviour. In the event, he found Valerie charming and delightful, and therefore she escaped his venom. To Alan he was mildly rude. "You're such a family man now" etc., Later, when he came with Rose and their two sons to live in a house near Land's End, the Lowndes became friendly and exchanged family visits with them. On these visits Roger and Alan drank a lot, which sometimes caused problems.

---

34 & 36 Valerie Lowndes

35 Michael Hunt

37 Karl Weschke (b.1925, Germany) came to England in 1945 as a P.O.W. On release he decided to pursue a career as an artist, coming to live in Cornwall in 1955, where he established friendships with artists including Bryan Wynter, Roger Hilton, Peter Lanyon and the poet W. S. Graham.

'MARCH FAIR'. *34 x 30 inches, oil on Board, 1960 (Private Collection)*

'BOY AND HIS DONKEY'. *24 x 30 inches, Oil on Canvas, 1950. Plate XX in the 1961 Exhibition Catalogue - see next page for details of the exhibition.*

In December 1961 Kalman held a Christmas exhibition that lasted until mid January. The exhibition was a great success and many pictures were sold. Andras Kalman, ever the showman, organised an accordion player for the opening and offered customers a large bowl of sausages with beer for the men and cider for the ladies. This attracted comment from several papers, the Evening Standard wrote, "An accordionist played in one corner. A tureen of hot sausages cooled in another." The exhibition attracted very positive mentions in most of the national newspapers, many of which made favourable comparisons with Lowry. A more perceptive Keith Sutton in the Listener wrote, "Whilst most of the art we see in London nowadays is the product of subtle and complex equations, every now and then we find an exhibition such as Alan Lowndes's at the Crane Kalman Gallery, which makes us think in terms of plain four square painting, and the critic begins to reach for a word like 'integrity' . . . He uses colour to intensify the mood all over the picture; areas are separated more by line than by tone. The movement and vivacity of his figures comes from their activities being related to one another in the literal sense rather than being aesthetically disposed around the picture."[38]

Nearly all the paintings in the exhibition depicted northern scenes or the circus, such as 'The Organ grinder', 'Street Corner' and 'Three Musical Clowns' and only four Cornish subjects. Amongst the sales, Kalman arranged a purchase of Alan's huge painting, 'Mealhouse Brow' by the Plymouth Art Gallery for £300.00.

'MEALHOUSE BROW', *Oil on Board, 1961, 64 x 52 inches bought by the Plymouth Art Gallery for £300.00 Plate 11 in the Catalogue*

The Kalman Gallery felt confident enough to suggest to Alan that in future the gallery should ask for and get over £100.00 for the medium sized pictures and more for the bigger ones; his painting of a snow scene had been priced at £175.00. The prices may look very modest nowadays, but only a few years before they had been selling for £10.00 in a gallery - progress indeed, and the pictures were selling

```
3 Clowns £75
High & Dry £110
Women Paddling £120
Bowls £100
Coronation St £135
Foggy Evening £38

Total.....£1,683
Framing of above £156
Sales - Framing £1,527

Your share £45

Cheque sent to you £78.19.9.
Full settlement to date.

(N.B. We have not included in this
account our expenses e.g.:
Catalogue £236.12.0
Colour Block £60
Other Blocks £62.8.3
Photos £6
Invtation cards £55.8.0
Party £110.0.)

Minus £400 paid as per contract..£1,127
```

Section from the accounts for the sale results of the 1961/1962 exhibition. It is remarkable to consider that 'Coronation Street' sold for only £135.00.

[38] 'Round the Art Galleries' by Keith Sutton, The Listener December 28th, 1961

ALAN IN THE TINNERS ARMS, ZENNOR 1961. *This photograph was featured in the catalogue of the 1961 exhibition opposite the Preface.*

'SHIP OFF ST. IVES',
9 x 12 inches, Oil on Board, 1962 (There is great confusion about the title of this painting, which appears under several guises)

'YELLOW BATHING SUIT', *18 x 22 inches Oil on Board, 1959*

'THE GAMBLERS', *40 x 30 inches, Oil on Board, 1962 (Collection of Bill Clark) Exhibited at the Osborne Gallery, New York, Catalogue Number 25*

'PLOVER COURT', 27 x 16.5 inches, Oil on Board, 1961, plate XXI in the 1961 Exhibition Catalogue

Mandy, Martin and Rosalind Lowndes

Details of:
Top Left: 'Mandy and Martin', 17 x 22 inches, Oil on Board, 1963 (Collection of Margaret Scarr)
Lower left: 'Mandy on Tonto', 14 x 18 inches Oil on Canvas, 1969 (Collection of the Artist)
Top Right: 'Ros on Pony', 10.5 x 13 inches, Oil on Board, 1965 (Collection of the Artist)
Lower Right: 'Ros by Flowers', 18 x 14 inches, Oil on Canvas, 1965 (Collection of the Artist)

In 1964 Alan and Valerie decided to move to a bigger house. There was no garden at 18 The Digey and nowhere for young children to play, except on the beach. There was also the constant battle to find suitable and cheap studio space. They soon found a tumble down larger property in Halestown not far from St. Ives. Halestown was a small housing development two miles southwest of St Ives, built for miners in the early 19th century by James Halse, Member of Parliament for St. Ives. He built the village in 1832, to house his mine workers. At that time the village was part of St. Ives Parish. There is a story that each house had just enough land to qualify the tenant for the right to vote, and only supporters of James Halse were selected as tenants.

Unfortunately they took the risky course of buying Ingledene in Halestown without selling 18 The Digey, which naturally created real financial hardship and a flurry of letters and phone calls between Alan, Kalman and the bank. Mr. Lane, the Manager of the District Bank in Knightsbridge gave them some very good advice and tried to persuade them to sell the Digey as soon as possible, otherwise interest payments on their loan to purchase the new house would swallow any proceeds from that sale, and, winter was upon them. He ended by thanking Alan for the picture he had given him of St. Ives Harbour.

With considerable help from Kalman, they eventually arranged a mortgage for the first time in their lives. "Alas it did not stop there, the house needed a great deal of money for improvements: there was no running water or electricity . . . In the sixties there were generous grants available to improve such properties. We got a lot of money towards it, but we still had to find a bit." They spent a great deal of time trying to arrange the work at the house, often in very difficult circumstances. Valerie was pregnant with Rosalind, and they did not own a car, so could only meet builders on site by taxi. Often the builder did not turn up for their appointments, just adding to the general nightmare. Eventually a new roof was built, a bathroom added and other constructional improvements made. Alan did much of the decoration himself, the children used to say "Oh dad's up there painting the doors."

The baby was due in June, but Valerie decided to stay in the Digey for the birth so that she could have Nurse Topham, who had delivered the other two babies. She rang Alan when she went into labour. He said, "I'll just finish these doors and then I'll come down, not to panic." "He was there in time, as he was with all the children. I was struggling with my first. I don't know how other mothers feel, but I mean I didn't have any consciousness of it being a baby, just this thing that was giving me pain. Alan said, 'Come on, give a push and think of all the nice clothes you will be able to wear when you are thin.' Do you know, that made me push. Alan was a great help towards all the births. We moved a week later."

Valerie had achieved what she wanted; she had a house with a garden and some space. Unfortunately the house was right next to the village pub. Mandy Lowndes remembers listening to the singing in the bar from her bedroom window. "On many occasions I remember being sent to fetch dad from the pub for mealtimes." Alan had obtained an Arts Council studio in St. Ives, and for the first and last time in his life commuted to work on the bus. After a short time they also acquired a car through the good offices of Andras Kalman swapping a painting for the car. This made all the difference in taking the children to school and shopping. 1964 was a very productive year for Alan, a new house, a new child and a large number of good paintings.

'ROSEWALL HILL'. *36 x 48 inches, Oil on Canvas, 1964 (Private Collection)*

PAGES OVER (134-135): DETAIL OF 'BEACH SCENE'. *32 x 48 inches, Oil on Board, October 1964 (Exhibited in the Tate Gallery, St. Ives, 'Porthmeor Beach: A Century of Images', April to October 1995.) Private Collection*

Lowndes painted some 35 pictures in 1964. Considering he moved house during the year and was involved in considerable decoration in his new home, it is very surprising what he achieved. Amongst his many paintings was one of his masterpieces on a large scale, 'Beach Scene' (illustrated on two previous pages) showing his skills at their very best. He has acutely observed the 'human on the beach' with gentle humour and a wonderful compositional organisation of the various typical figures seen on any British beach. Their very ordinariness has given the picture a visual dynamism that is extraordinary. He has managed to avoid all the pitfalls of glitzy commercial beach scenes that abound in any seaside area and many galleries.

Kalman had previously written to Alan on the 12th of August, 1963: he was to have an exhibition in New York. Kalman's plan was to exhibit "both your Manchester and St. Ives work, especially those of St. Ives which - you may not be aware of it yet - have a link with Northern work (i.e. the woman with the shopping bag walking along the beach, 'The West Pier', 'Painter and Critics')." Unfortunately Lowndes never really felt part of the exhibition: Kalman made all the arrangements without involving Alan at all, other than informing him of the exhibition itself. Nevertheless it was a great fillip for him to have an exhibition in such a prestigious city. After the show had finished, Alan wrote to Kalman, "A letter arrived from the New York Gallery - very pleasant in tone. He said that you had all the press cuttings. I'd like to see them sometime."

12th August 1963.

Dear Alan,

New York, Madison Avenue, here I come! You have a show laid on in New York in a gallery which is opening in the autumn there. They seem to be nice people, not with the conventional gallery outlook.

18 the Digey
Aug 15th

Dear Andre,
Madison Ave ahoy! The whole idea about the Gallery and the Follow up Exhibitions is terriffic! I shall be coming up sometime next week and will bring some work up with me. Valerie who at present is in Sheffield with the Children might join me for a day or two in London
Will be ringing you up soon
Love to all
Alan

Alan's first reaction to the news of a New York exhibition and at the following one at the Rutland Gallery was very positive, but there was little contact with him about the exhibition, and he later felt as if the exhibition was nothing to do with him.

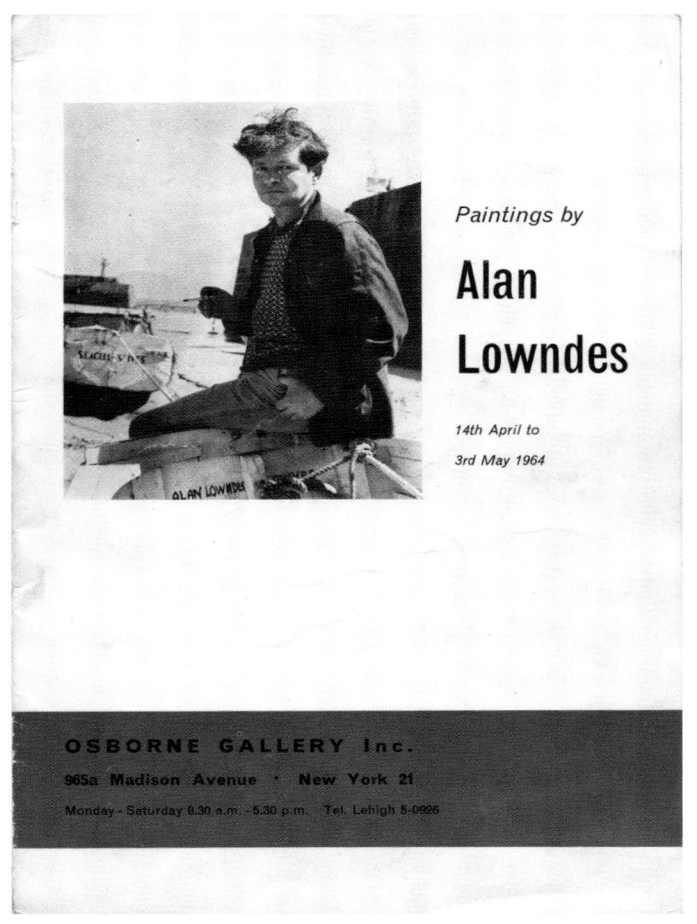

TELLING THE TALE 1964 32" × 21½" oil on board

TWO IN A BAR 1963 30" × 20" oil on board

ENTERING THE CIRCUS 1963 39½" × 32" oil on canvas

SEAGULLS 1963 48" × 30" oil on canvas

Pages from the Osborne Gallery catalogue. April 14th – May 3rd, 1964. New York
The Paintings, 'Telling the Tale' and 'Entering the Circus' belong to the Arts Council of Great Britain and were featured in the recent travelling exhibition 'Unpopular Culture' curated by Grayson Perry.

Detail of 'Telling the Tale', 21.5 x 32 inches, Oil on Canvas, 1964 (Collection of the Arts Council) Exhibited at the Osborne Gallery, New York, 1964, Catalogue Number 23

'ENTERING THE CIRCUS'. 39.5 x 32 inches, Oil on Canvas, 1963 (Collection of the Arts Council) Exhibited at the Osborne Gallery, New York, 1964, Catalogue Number 27

LEFT: PRESS COMMENT AFTER THE EXHIBITIONS IN NEW YORK AND LONDON, 1964

LIST OF PAINTINGS EXHIBITED AT THE OSBORNE GALLERY

Life was becoming more comfortable for the family. With more space at home, the Lowndes were able to host bigger parties at least three to four times a year on birthdays or Christmas. These parties went well and were much appreciated by their guests. They were also able to put up more visitors - Alan's siblings and their families or Valerie's family and friends. Between visitors, they offered a B. & B. service letting two rooms. As Valerie had never been able to fry an egg properly, Alan did all these in a large frying pan and added them to her full English breakfast.

In the mid sixties a new feature entered Alan's life, he became a member of the Chelsea Arts Club. An artist friend suggested that Alan should join, as the accommodation was friendlier and cheaper than hotels. He did this and was delighted to find the accommodation to be a large old house in Old Church Street, which felt like home from home. He already knew one or two members and soon came to know others. At that time the club was men-only, but later, when women were allowed, Valerie accompanied him for overnight stays. She too enjoyed the comfortable amenities, good food and friendly atmosphere. However financial worries were still paramount, as the letter from Andras Kalman on the 18th of May 1965 illustrates.

```
                                   18th May 1965

Alan Lowndes, Esq.,
55 Halsetown,
St. Ives,
Cornwall.


Dear Alan,
           I have got your two letters, in which you ask
the yearly allowance should be increased to £1,500.

           Well, I just can't do it, Alan. I shall make
a compromise and say that the £1,000 bankers order will
stay as it is and during the year I will make an additional
purchase for £250.

           If I gave you £1,500 a year and I sold £1,750
worth of your pictures per year, my benefit on these sales
would be £250, and with the bank rate and the overhead
this would be nil.

           I never stopped you from trying to sell, (even
below our London prices, i.e. 15 to 20% lower would be
reasonable, otherwise you would cut your own market).
Therefore, I would suggest that you could try and sell
£250 to £400 of your pictures in St. Ives, but I would
like you to keep us informed to whom and for how much,
as we did the same to you.

           I have only just got back and I will work out with
the accountants what are the total sales made since our last
report of sales.
           I hope you and the family are well.
                      Love to you, Valerie and the children,


P.S. I will inform Mr. Pollard about this.
```

LEFT: *There are many letters such as this concerning Alan's constant and understandable request for a bigger annual retainer. It is interesting that Kalman is happy with Alan selling from the studio.*

Denis Bowen, Director of the New Vision Gallery, was the leader of avant-garde art in Britain, especially informal abstraction.[39] As well as being an outstanding painter himself, he showed many of the famous artists from Cornwall, who were quite unknown, when Denis first exhibited their works. He was invited with Kenneth Coutts-Smith to stay with Nancy Wynne-Jones at Trevaylor, a large house near Madron, which she had bought in 1964, to meet Barbara Hepworth and Ben Nicholson. Kenneth Coutts-Smith, a fellow director of the New Vision Gallery, was author of the Dream of Icarus, a survey of post war British art. He was also a remarkable character with many talents, and even at times worked on the fishing smacks in Cornwall. They went along to a studio in St. Ives to meet a painter about whom they had heard a great deal, Alan Lowndes. They went in some trepidation; Denis had been warned that Alan could be 'difficult', but Denis found him very helpful and friendly.

After a few rather unproductive months, Alan wrote to Kalman in January apologising for lack of work. "Sorry I haven't sent any work up as promised. The stuff I had ready I reviewed and now I have to finish and re-do some all over again. Maybe some sort of psychological block although I don't usually go in for that sort of thing." One can just imagine what Kalman thought of all this. Fortunately Andras Kalman was able to help

---

[39] New Vision grew out of meetings, discussions and displays of work that Denis initiated with his students in 1951. In 1955 a permanent exhibition space was opened by Denis, Frank Avray-Wilson, Halima Nalacz and, later, Ken Coutts-Smith at 4 Seymour Place, Marble Arch, where it remained until 1966. Denis was not the only founder or director, but he was the only one to remain fully involved for the life of the gallery.

financially, especially with good sales of Alan's paintings.

One afternoon, Alan returned from his studio in a particularly drunken state. He agreed with Valerie that he should build a studio at home to assist in keeping temptation away. Most surprisingly Alan completed his studio in the garden very quickly. In his home studio he was able to paint all day with coffee and tea breaks interspersed by his lunchtime session in the Halestown Inn. Whilst he was working on the premises, he could bring an almost finished painting into the house and hang it up in the living room, where he would study it for several days. Then he would take it back to the studio for any alterations and place it back on the wall for further study. This would be repeated several times before he signed and dated a painting as a finished work. This procedure indicates how serious Lowndes was about his paintings, and should help dismiss the thoughtless comments about Lowndes 'the naïve painter'. He was a very serious painter indeed, whatever he might have said socially.

In 1969 when all the children were at school, Alan painted two nudes of Valerie in their garden. It was a very secluded garden, and the weather must have been hot and settled. Every afternoon for several days Alan worked assiduously on both of these paintings. Valerie simply took up the pose and changed sides at half time. Alan was very pleased with these pictures when they were finished. (See 'Nude and Fig Tree' on the opposite page) By now Breon O'Casey was Chairman of the Penwith Society and had started inviting the senior painters in the area to show in the Society's exhibitions. Alan sent the large frontal nude, 'The Sunbather' to the next show, which was bought by the photographer Cornel Lucas. Cornel told the author that Lowndes often used to come to his photographic studio to enjoy liquid refreshment and stay long after he was welcome. In the end, Cornel hid any alcohol he might have when Alan hove into sight. Valerie still owns the second nude.

The mid and late sixties were good painting times for Alan; he completed many impressive pictures during this period.

'BEACH SCENE', *16 x 12 inches, Oil on Board, 1963 (Private Collection)*

Right: 'The Old Organ Grinder', 22 x 18 inches, Acrylic on Canvas, 1963

'Nude and Fig Tree', Oil on Canvas, 22 x 30 inches, 1969 (Collection of the Artist)

TOP: 'STORMY SUNSET'. 20 x 30 inches, Oil on Canvas. 1965 (Private Collection)

BELOW: 'A WATERY SUNSET'. 24 x 36 inches, Oil on Canvas, 1965 Exhibited at the Tate Gallery, St. Ives in a mixed exhibition, 1997 (Private Collection)

'Serene Sunset'. *36 x 48 inches, Oil on Canvas, 1965*

LEFT: 'SHOOTING RANGE',
12 x 14 inches, Oil on
Board, 1967 (Private
Collection)

'A VILLAGE SCHOOL', 20 x 30 inches, Acrylic on Board, 1965 (Private Collection) "It is almost certainly Halsetown Village School, which I attended for my first primary year." Mandy McCann (née Lowndes)

RIGHT: 'THE BIG CHIMNEY', *12 x 6 inches, Acrylic on Board, 1967 (Collection of the Artist)*

'THREE BOATS', *18 x 15 inches, Oil on Board, 1966*

Chapter 9 - Cornwall Part 2 - Aspects of Life, Art and Drinking in Cornwall until 1970

The Lowndes were expanding their social circle, particularly when their children attended Nancledra School. John and Judi Emmanuel had three children in the school; Donald and Elizabeth Swann had two children there. Pat and Anne Dolan lived out on the moors not far away, old friends, but now more accessible, as were Michael and Margaret Snow.[40] The wives used to go to each other's houses after school for the little ones to play and the mothers to gossip. Life could be lonely for the wife of an artist. The Grahams were fortunate to have a 'taxi' account opened for them by Nancy Wynne-Jones to enable them to visit friends such as the Lowndes from time to time. Usually they would come early in the evening, spend an hour or so with the children before going with Alan to the Halestown Inn. The landlord, Alex Pope, was a retired opera singer. Sydney Graham had a powerful tenor voice and fancied himself as a singer. He and the landlord got on well. As ever, Alan and Sydney could fall out with each other all too easily, but just as easily they became friends again. Two letters from Sydney illustrate their relationship well.

Alan and Valerie started to attend Sunday services at Zennor church on a regular basis. The vicar, The Reverend Hitchens, discovered that Valerie had not been confirmed and arranged for her to be included in the next batch for confirmation. All their children were christened in the church. The same group of friends came to each christening, Nancy, Boots, Sydney, Nessie, Tony, Mr. and Mrs. Holmes and a few others. Later they transferred their allegiance to St. John's in the Fields in St. Ives. The new vicar, John Harper and his family had moved into a house in Halestown. St. John's was much nearer than Zennor, only a mile away at the top of the Stennack and was also much livelier with a full congregation every Sunday. "John Harper was a stern vicar. If ever we missed a service, he was at the front door. 'Where were you?' We seldom missed a service."[41] Alan had a good tenor singing voice and was irritated by Valerie's inability to sing hymns in tune. "You keep changing the key."

PAGE LEFT (148):
'TWO OLD CRONIES',
18 x 14 inches, Gouache, 1963
(Collection of Manya Igel)

40 John Emmanuel, painter born in Bury 1930. Moved to Cornwall 1964 and has exhibited widely locally and in the UK. Donald Swann, painter, still active in Cornwall. Pat Dolan - see page 177. Michael Seward Snow, b. Manchester 1930. Professional painter, sculptor and designer and friend of Sydney Graham. Snow Exhibited with Penwith Society 1953-65, Rowan Gallery, London and elsewhere. Directed the Combined Honours degree courses offered by Exeter University until 1985. Michael and his wife Margaret, an English teacher, became executors of Sydney Graham's estate.
41 Valerie Lowndes

Alan, the Family Man

Far Left: Alan and Tom Hassell, St. Ives, 1960s

Centre: Alan, Valerie and Amanda, Land's End, 1960s

Right: Valerie, Alan and Antonia Hassell 1960s

One of Alan's favourite places in Cornwall was Land's End. When the children were all at school, he and Valerie used to drive there; the place was completely undeveloped then. They would walk along the cliff tops or just sit on the grass and enjoy the peace of it all, the only sound being the cry of gulls. They just looked at the colours, the movement of the sea, the lighthouse and the occasional ship passing. Alan as usual did many drawings. "There is a large painting called 'Land's End' and probably others from these sketches."[42]

About this time camping holidays on the continent were becoming popular. Longing to see France again, Valerie suggested the idea to Alan, only to be met with a blunt refusal. He had spent six years in a tent in the army, and nothing on earth would drag him under canvas again, that was final. Valerie was obviously upset at his attitude and was grumbling to a friend about Alan's reaction. Her friend replied, "Don't worry, my husband was just the same. I simply told him that the children and I were going camping in France, and he was welcome to come along, if he liked." Valerie took this excellent advice and informed Alan she was going to France with the children and he was welcome to come. For once he was speechless with anger, and relations between the two were so severely strained, they hardly spoke for weeks.

Meanwhile Valerie booked the ferry and made all the requisite arrangements for camping. Alan came of course. Once established in a French campsite, he realised it was nothing like army camping. The family had a very happy holiday in Normandy and went on several other camping holidays in France. When they returned to Cornwall, he told friends how wonderful his camping holiday had been and tried to persuade their non-camping friends to try one. "It's a bit like marriage," he said, "once you are in it yourself you want everyone else to suffer." Valerie hoped he was joking.

"Lowndes is a greater painter than Lowry." Sir Terry Frost (1915 - 2006)

Alan had become good friends with one of the best artists in the area, Terry Frost. Terry lived just round the corner from the Digey making contact for the two families very easy. The Frosts were to remain friends for the rest of Alan's life, not least because the two men had a mutual respect for each other's ability as painters. Later, the parents and children of the two families often met for great Sunday family gatherings.

Terry had a genuine admiration for Alan's paintings and vice versa. Though Terry was abstract in style and Alan figurative, he could appreciate the brilliance of Alan's composition and observation of people. He told Giovanni Tieuli, a Venetian friend and glass maker, that he could look at any Alan Lowndes painting and recognise all the people in it, even if they had their backs to him, so exact was his observation of the way they moved and held themselves. He considered Alan to be a very sensitive painter, who managed to capture the tiniest details without actually painting them. Leonardo da Vinci once wrote that Giotto was a great painter because he had drawn from nature and had not learned from masters. Alan had the remarkable gift of true observation of looking at people and places.

42 Valerie Lowndes (See pages 152 and 153 for an illustration of 'Land's End')

Anthony Frost, Terry's son, commented: "I knew Alan since I was a little lad. I didn't go out drinking with him or anything like that, I left that to dad. I remember driving him back from a party once in his car, a little blue thing, my knees were under my chin, it was so small. All the way back he was chuntering on about what he had read in the Guardian. My dad always said he was the best-read man he had ever met, he knew everything. He was constantly quoting things, which made you jealous in a way.

My memories of Alan were mainly when I was travelling backwards and forwards from College in Cardiff. I would stop off at Alan's house in Upper Cam. I had my sketchbook on one occasion and showed it to him. He picked out all the drawings I was unsure about, they were figurative then. He made me feel great, he told me 'what wonderful observation' I had shown. He taught me the very valuable lesson that what I thought was a doodle was far more important than a drawing I had laboured over and considered much more major. He could see the observation in them.

That has stuck with me for evermore. I have always loved Alan's work. At first because Dad loved it, but gradually I came to appreciate it for myself. I really like that true honest figurative painting. It is what is taken out that is important: he just left the essentials. He often paints pictures with people with their backs to you, but it leads you to make the story for yourself. I don't know how he did it: he takes things out and puts them where he wants them to be to make the painting work. It was fantastic the way he would look at things and select just what he wanted. He often over painted to achieve exactly what he wanted."

Anthony has put into words the feelings of so many people that appreciate Alan's work, his wonderful compositional sense and observation of people and places. Far too often he has been dismissed as a naïve painter, without any reference to the studied and intellectual way he composed the image he was portraying, let alone his vast width of reading and general knowledge. Alan had a genius's way of transposing what he saw as a composition on canvas. He could depict places and people, their emotions, foibles, humour and sadness by placing them in exactly the right place with the right colours and backgrounds. He extracted anything extraneous to his concept leaving the viewer with what appears a 'simple' scene, but is it? A 'Lowndes' painting deserves many viewings before the full story actually appears. He is certainly figurative, but it is a kind of abstracted figuration leaving much for the imagination and viewer's curiosity. A figurative painter has to make exactly the same decisions as an abstract painter. Above all, Alan knew what to leave out.

Anthony Frost in his beautiful studio in Penzance with Alan Lowndes's brushes

"I was given Alan's brushes by Valerie. Unfortunately they are terrible, there is nothing left on them. I don't know how he painted with them."

PAGES OVER (152-153): DETAIL OF 'THE LAND'S END', 30 x 50 inches, Oil on Board, 1970

Terry Frost was interviewed by Sue Lawley in Desert Island Disks on the radio in 1998. He stated that, "Many people consider Alan Lowndes to be a naïve painter, he wasn't, he was a great painter." Anthony Frost was insistent that his father wanted to ensure that any biography should include his comment that 'Lowndes was a greater painter than Lowry'. "My Dad picked a painting by Alan to be exhibited in his exhibition at the Tate, 'Painting not Painting', 8th February 2003 - 11th May 2003, at St. Ives. The picture was of a man painting a lovely big boat." The title of the painting was 'The Painter and Critics', 1964. The picture was actually exhibited in 'Artists on Artists' exhibition at the Tate at the same time as 'Painting not Painting'. Terry and Alan temporarily shared a studio in St. Ives and decided to paint the same scene of men painting boats. Both have captured the essentials of the occasion without extraneous detail. It would be simple to recognise the three men in Alan's painting, so well has he caught their individual postures and movements.

'Painter and Critics', 36 x 48 inches, Oil on Canvas, 1963 (Collection of Dr. and Mrs. Jack Harris) Exhibited at the Osborne, Gallery, New York 1964, 14-04-64 to 03-05-64.

"Terry chose Alan's painting to be part of an 'Artist on Artists' display along with other works from the Tate collection that had inspired him, it was one of the works he was most keen to have in the show. Alan had chosen the colours that Terry was using for the boat hulls and framed the hulls to replicate forms in Terry's work as part of a joke to wind him up. Terry loved it. I think they may have been sharing a studio at the time." Martin Bolton, The Tate Gallery

Anthony Frost continued. "Alan makes the painting look easy, as if there is not a lot in there, but there is a lot in there. It is what he has left out and pared it down to that makes the painting so good. It is a very difficult thing to do. I know as a painter you are always trying to put too much in. His intellectual knowledge was part of this, his keen observation. That is the essence of his painting."

ABOBE: TERRY FROST: 'RED CIRCLE AND BLACK'. *48 x 48 inches, Oil on Canvas, 1963 (Collection of Dr. and Mrs. Jack Harris)*

A number of critics have asserted that the backgrounds of Alan's paintings were often textured in a way reminiscent of his decorating days. Anthony Frost remembered the flesh pink colour that he used and pushed around the painting more to change the shapes of the objects and get the space better. He often used a lovely meridian green and a crimson red for the same reasons, rather than a 'decorator's' effect. "He made those lovely colour decisions, I don't know if they were true to life, but they were exactly right for the painting." He used thick oil paint or acrylic to add texture and atmosphere, but equally he could paint in watercolour or gouache.

Art critics are fond of attributing influences of other painters on artists' work and organising them into schools or groups, they just love labels. Alan stood out in Cornwall being a figurative painter surrounded by abstract painters, and many of them regarded him as 'old fashioned' or 'out of date'. To his dying day, he felt resentful of their criticism. It must have been very difficult for him with the enormous volume of abstract art pouring out of Cornwall and much of it mediocre in the extreme. Some critics have suggested Alan was influenced by Christopher Wood and Alfred Wallis, which seems somewhat strange, as Alan's style was well developed long before he came to Cornwall or saw their work. There is no doubt that he admired them as painters, but that is all. He admired the work of Alfred Wallis above all, especially his compositional brilliance. He said that he only had to paint a boat and/or a harbour for Alfred Wallis to be mentioned. He thought Wallis was a great painter, who sadly never knew how good he really was.

During his lifetime Alan felt he had been forgotten in the mass of abstraction in Cornwall, but other artists were inspired by his work. Simeon Stafford (b. 1956), working away in Cornwall, undeservedly has been ignored until recently. His zany, colourful and beautifully executed paintings have started to gain considerable recognition, as the public has become more aware of his work. Simeon regards Alan as an artist who greatly influenced his approach to composition and has painted several pictures in homage to him. Recently he has completed a number of paintings under the general title of 'The Lowndes Series'.

'Fish and Chips', by Simeon Stafford. *18 x 24 inches, oil on canvas, painted 11-05-2007. "The fish and chip shop has been attributed as being on Lowndes Street as a bit of fun. In the 'Chip Shop' I am following the way Lowndes painted figures with the back drop of buildings below the roof line. I of course loved the way he applied his paint and the effects he achieved." Simeon Stafford, 2007*

As we have seen, many people have completely disregarded how much intellectual consideration he gave a painting before commencing and during the execution of the work itself. Lowndes wrote that most painting was slogging hard work, though sometimes he felt he received a gift from God, and the picture almost painted itself. The Painter, Bob Crossley, once had a discussion with Alan about the importance of painting. He asked Alan the question:

"Which is more important, people or painting?"
"Painting"

Unfortunately his drinking habits were causing concern to Andras Kalman. He would arrive by train at the Kalman gallery in Knightsbridge, drop his bag at the entrance and leave saying "See you in 10 minutes, must have something to eat." Four hours later he would reappear from the 'Bunch of Grapes' completely drunk. It was becoming difficult to know how to handle him. Conversely sometimes, Alan or Alan with Valerie would arrive and be asked to come back in an hour or so, Andras was busy with a client. When they came back, Andras was still busy. This had been known to go on for three days. The Bunch of Grapes across the road was a good refuge.

Life was not entirely smooth in the Lowndes household. Slim Ingram describes a visit to Alan in Halestown with his wife Jill and her father Sam Junior, Alan's eldest brother, for a week's holiday in the sixties; the exact date is not known. "In those days the journey from Stockport to St. Ives was an adventure in itself - breakfast on Bodmin Moor after an all night drive and all that." On his arrival at Alan's house, he was very surprised at the number of dustbins of wine fermenting, especially his rice wine. Slim found it disgusting to drink, but Alan seemed oblivious to the taste. Slim recalls that each day was exactly the same. They would all be sitting down for breakfast and enjoying a cup of coffee. Alan would arrive, take off one of the dustbin lids and take a drink. "That was the start of it, that could be 9 o'clock in the morning. We presumed he carried on during the rest of the day." Slim and his wife, Jill, would go out for the day to the beach or somewhere else to keep out of the way. On their return they would have dinner at about 6 p.m. at which they were offered the 'dustbin' wine. Sam didn't like wine and his wife, Mae, didn't drink, they were thus saved from having to imbibe his terrible concoctions. Once the meal was over, Alan would say, "We are off out."

Slim felt obliged to accompany him to keep the family happy, because the rest of them 'did not want to know'. "During the week we were there, we never failed to find a pub with a lock in, a Northern expression for the pub being open. We drank all evening and fell into bed as soon as we reached home. Alan seemed to come alive the moment we left the house and knew we were going to a pub. His appearance was quite dramatic with his trilby hat dipped down over the side of his face Svengali style; his eyes sparkled and his face became all bubbly. It was as if he wanted a family, but preferred to be a bachelor to be free to do what he wanted. It was a section of his life that was his and away from everything else he did. I have often wondered why he was able to relax so much in the pub. I think he was never quite sure of his talent. He painted pictures, but it did not swell over into him as a person." There is no doubt Alan became a different man in a pub. This was his life, and Slim has touched on Alan's major problem, he was very insecure and used drink as a social vehicle, sadly the volume of his consumption destroyed his life.

"The last painting I saw him do was a nude of his wife, Valerie. He painted my wife Jill three times. One of them was owned by Charles Laughton." Slim was also very surprised at the fractious atmosphere in the house. "Alan was quarrelling all the time with Sam; even though Alan looked up to Sam as a father figure, the two brothers were really antagonistic to each other. He and Valerie were also constantly bickering. If I had been driving my own car, I would have driven home later the first day. Jill and I spent much of the time trying to keep out of the unpleasant atmosphere." However, later when the family had serious problems after Alan's death, Sam could not have been more helpful to Valerie and the children.

Bob Bourne, a very impecunious figurative painter, was always receiving the bitter side of Alan's tongue entirely because of his accent; he had attended Eton. Sam Senior, Alan's father, had ingrained into him a resentful attitude to people whom he considered to be of a higher class than himself. It never occurred to Alan that Bob had no money or other financial support. Bob thought Alan was always bitter about Andras Kalman making a profit from his paintings, because Kalman never gave him any information about the prices at which he sold his pictures. "All the talk in the Sloop was about abstract art. Figurative artists were not part of the conversation. I felt Alan always had a chip on his shoulder, he was small and working class."[43]

Increasingly Alan, the kind and amusing man, was being replaced by a more truculent person. Many a time Valerie had to smooth ruffled feathers the following day. At this time a serious event occurred for a number of their friends. Nancy Wynne-Jones had been courted by an Irishman, Conor Fallon. She announced that she was going to marry Conor, brother of the art critic Brian Fallon. Once married in 1966, Conor was not so keen on keeping all the hangers-on that Nancy had been supporting, which affected Sydney and Nessie Graham most of all, who were given notice to vacate 'The Little House' in favour of Conor's parents. There was an outcry. The Grahams had no regular income to rent anywhere else, this would have left them homeless. After much agitation by a number of people, especially Bryan Wynter, Nancy procured a cottage for them at Madron, where Sydney and Nessie lived the rest of their lives. Her old friend, Boots Redgrave, Tony O'Malley and Bill Featherstone were also asked to leave. It was particularly difficult for Boots Redgrave, she and Nancy had almost been as close as sisters.

From left to right:

Alan & Valerie Lowndes, Sam Lowndes Junior, Conor Fallon, Nancy Wynne-Jones, Mandy, Martin and Rosalind Lowndes.

43 Bob Bourne

Alan's drinking was still causing major tensions within his household. All the family money was being spent on alcohol, not on the basics of food and clothing. This of course led to fearful rows between Valerie and Alan about money. He refused to budget causing immense problems for Valerie to meet household bills. He simply would not put aside so much for gas, electricity and food, "then you can have a pound a day to spend." Alan's response was always along the lines, 'I'm not going to live like that. If I meet anybody and he wants to take me for a drink, I've got to buy one back you know, and that's what happens.' Valerie and the family used to joke that whenever he passed the Sloop, an invisible hand would come out and drag him in.

Even in his parlous financial state, Alan could be a very generous man. "He caught the morning bus into town and returned on the five o'clock bus, if he hadn't been caught up with friends. Somehow on a Friday he would bring a present for all the children. He was generous with his hospitality for friends and family." Mandy Lowndes recalled a 'special' present, ". . . Dad had just returned from one of his trips to London to see Andras. It was a big thing in those days going up to London from Cornwall, and he often brought presents back for us kids when he returned from these trips, so there was an air of expectation. However nothing was immediately forthcoming, and I think one of us asked him if he had brought anything back. At which he went off and came back with a package, which he placed on the table. We gathered excitedly round, wondering what this could be. He opened it up with a look of glee, pulled out a large jar and exclaimed with great relish, "Mustard." Of course our faces dropped, it was a bit of a let down, as none of us had the slightest interest in mustard . . . He obviously thought it was a bit of a coup."

Though Alan was living in Cornwall, he was still painting many northern scenes. He found it easier to paint what he knew so well, rather than the 'new' surroundings in Halestown. He tried to visit Stockport once a year, but did not always manage to do so; also his trips north became less frequent when he lost his Stockport studio. On one northern visit in 1968 he supported Slim Ingram's improvements at the Neptune Theatre in Liverpool by showing some of his paintings in the theatre's first ever exhibition in its new little art gallery on September 26th. The council owned the theatre and organised a grand civic reopening. Rather aptly the play they saw was Ibsen's 'Enemy of the People'.

The theatre manager, Theresa Collard, who had the 'gift of the gab', told Alan how much she liked one of his paintings; he just gave it to her as a present. Slim commented, "That was just like Alan, he didn't put a value on anything." Valerie justifiably claims that Slim was quite wrong. Alan was fully aware of his worth, and this act was just a theatrical front. In a letter to Trevor Nunn dated 9th of January, 1978 Alan wrote the following words, "I have to take people's reactions to what I do on their say so. One of my rewards is to meet people who've had my works for years and still like them. What I am saying is I suppose you don't have to bore the pants off people just because your work is bracketed as 'culture'." He must have been pleased when Bill Naughton, the writer and playwright, wrote on the 8th of March, 1976, "There's something about your pictures, Alan, which grows on you the more you see them. They get brighter instead of dimming."

Alan stayed with Slim for a week during the Neptune exhibition. He took the opportunity to meet some of his old friends, particularly Roger McGough, poet, writer and successful singer with Scaffold, the painter, Adrian Henri and the poet and sculptor, Arthur Dooley. Slim accompanied Alan in his meetings with them and was most surprised by the esteem in which they held him. During these visits, Alan was very saddened to see the changes wrought by councils, developers and planners to the Stockport area, his 'home'. Nevertheless he continued to paint his northern scenes all the time he lived in Cornwall or elsewhere. Alan's exhibition at the Neptune Theatre contained some of his very best paintings, including one of his masterpieces, 'Painter and Critics'. On the next page a copy of his exhibition list is illustrated, after which are examples of his work exhibited at the Neptune Theatre and elsewhere at that time.

```
NEPTUNE THEATRE EXHIBITION

        HANOVER STREET

           LIVERPOOL


       A L A N   L O W N D E S

 1.  Painter and Critics  1963
 2.  Seagulls             1963
 3.  The Gamblers         1962
 4.  Mum Sweeping         1963
 5.  Mill Street          1956
 6.  Six Dustbins         1961
 7.  Cornwall
 8.  The Betting Shop
 9.  A Quiet Smoke
10.  Demolishing Lancashire Hill   1966
11.  Great Howard Street           1960
12.  Formby Street                 1960
13.  The Slipway                   1957
14.  Little Girl                   1965
15.  Top Lane Halsetown            1967
16.  Demolishing Nicholson Arms    1966
17.  Piccadilly Lost Property      1963
18.  Waiting Their Turn            1967
19.  Paddy's Brow                  1968
20.  A & R Mill                    1968

         Prices on application
```

LEFT: COPY OF THE LIST OF PAINTINGS FOR SALE IN THE EXHIBITION OF ALAN'S WORK IN THE NEPTUNE THEATRE, LIVERPOOL SEPTEMBER 26TH, 1968

'PADDY'S BROW', *18 x 14 inches, Acrylic on Board, 1968*

RIGHT: 'THE ANCIENT MARINER'. *24 x 20 inches, Oil on Canvas, 1968*

'THE SNACK WAGGON'. *16 x 20 inches, Acrylic on Board, 1968 (Collection of the Crane Kalman Gallery)*

161

'AR Mill', *14 x 10 inches, Oil on Board, 1968*

Page Right (163): Detail of 'Chestergate', *20 x 16 inches, Oil on Canvas, 1968 (Collection of the Crane Kalman Gallery)*

Debts were becoming more and more serious. Valerie finally wrote to Andras to explain the situation on February 1st, 1967. She apologised that she was writing not Alan and then outlined in detail her weekly costs against her weekly income, which showed a fairly large imbalance. She also pointed out that they hardly ever went out and hadn't had a holiday for over six years. She asked him if he could raise their annual allowance from £1000.00 to £1500.00. Andras replied on the 21st stating that he was unable in present market conditions to raise the allowance. However he said he would buy some more of Alan's paintings for himself. He also urged Alan to take a job to augment his income and paint two or three days a week. As he pointed out, there are "no more than twenty painters in the country who can live entirely by their work."

Alan wrote to Andras on February 23rd apologising for Valerie's letter and explained how she did not fully understand art accounts. Valerie and he were considering selling their house to move north; the St. Ives area had gone to pot - almost literally. "All the real painters have gone and just amateurs and potters are left." He was unwilling to attempt to obtain a job, as he was 46 years old, untrained and would not be able to compete with much younger and qualified people. He hoped Valerie could find a job in a couple of years when the children had grown up, but he was unwilling to jettison "the years put into painting as it's always been my maxim that if one perseveres it will amount to something. Indeed it already has in that we live well by the normal standards." He claimed that, "Women like to have things cut and dried little realising the elasticity of things as they are ... Women in my view or experience like to see it down on paper and in the bank. I have seen the market for paintings down here drying up with the absence of the right type of visitors to the area. At least in the north I met outright rejection or acceptance." His financial logic must have made Valerie so frustrated and upset. It could only be a matter of time before she would be forced to take action against his totally unrealistic approach.

In the period 1968 to 1970 many of their friends - the Wynters, Tony O'Malley and Boots Redgrave - moved out of town. The old circle had completely broken up, the Frosts had moved to Banbury in 1963, the Mitchells were in Newlyn and Pat Dolan was now in Cardiff. Brian Wall and Bill Featherstone had gone to America. Willie Barnes-Graham spent more time in Scotland. Peter Lanyon had died in 1964. The winters were long in Cornwall, and life started to become dull. Financial problems were piling up, and the family situation was becoming very hard. Alan was still as irresponsible as ever with 'I'm a painter, why should I worry about mundane things like money?' attitude. In 1970 Valerie finally decided enough was enough and gave Alan an ultimatum - she was leaving with the children, either he came with them or he stayed behind, that was entirely up to him. Alan had the good sense to leave Cornwall with his wife and three children.

The last few years had been a very difficult time for the family with deep financial and alcohol related stress. Nevertheless Alan produced some magnificent paintings during those last years. However drunk or troubled he could become, he never lowered his standard of painting at this time. It was a very different story for Valerie, she had to cope with feeding and clothing the family with debts mounting up in every way

PAGE LEFT (164): 'THE PORTWOOD BRIDGE', *30 x 20 inches, Oil on canvas, 1968 (Private Collection)*

PAGES OVER (166-167): DETAIL OF 'SETTING UP STALLS', *30 x 50 inches, Oil on Canvas, 1969 (Collection of the Crane Kalman Gallery)*

'ROSEWALL HILL IN WINTER', 20 x 24 inches, Oil on Canvas, 1969 (Collection of Bill Clark)
Snow was a rarity in Cornwall, and Alan seized the chance to paint it.

'Man, Cat and Boat', 24 x 30 inches, Oil on Canvas, 1969 (Private Collection)

Pages Over (170-171): Detail of 'Champ and Challenger', 36 x 48 inches, Oil on Canvas, 1969 (Private Collection) Formerly in the collection of Sir Michael Parkinson

SIR MICHAEL PARKINSON *featured at home with 'Champ and Challenger' hanging behind him.*

'THE GOAL KICK', *20 x 16 inches, Oil on Board, 1969 (Private Collection)*

'St. Ives harbour'. *11 x 15 inches, Oil on Board, 1969*

'THE SURPRISE ATTACK', *9 x 6 inches, Oil on Board, 1970 (Private Collection)*

'PZ 63' (St. Ives Harbour). 30 x 40 inches. Oil on Board. 1970 (Collection of Bill Clark)

'COMING HOME, CHRISTMAS EVE', 20 x 30 inches, Oil on Canvas, 1969 ("...the way in which the snowballers have punched white bullet holes by their cyclist victim; whatever the device it makes a point which nobody else would have seen in the same way." John Willett)

Chapter 10 - Gloucestershire, 1970 to 1975

Valerie had made a decision to move, but where? In the end the family compromised on Upper Cam, a village near Dursley in Gloucestershire. They bought Bloomfield House opposite the beautiful fourteenth century St. John's Church in 1970. They nearly bought a large old house with a lovely studio on the top floor, but in hopeless condition. 'Bloomfield' was very convenient, the children could walk to school, the house was not too far from the Frosts at Banbury, and London and Cornwall were within reach. Most importantly for both of them, the sale of the big house in Halestown cleared their debts. Valerie was also able to enjoy a separate income at a good job nearby. She was pleased. Sydney Graham was a long way away. Alan would have less temptation to drink.

BLOOMFIELD HOUSE, the Lowndes' first house in Upper Cam, Gloucestershire, opposite St. John's Church.

Valerie explained:

"We had expected to be lonely at first, but this was not so. Rosalind immediately made friends with the neighbours' children, and so we met the parents, Pam and Aled Pugh, who became good friends. A welcome surprise was the discovery that Banbury was only 50 miles away, so we could now visit the Frosts easily. Cardiff, where two old friends from Cornwall, Pat Dolan[44] and Alan Wood[45], were teaching at the Art College, was only an hour's drive in the opposite direction. These two and their wives, and the Woods' son, became regular weekend visitors. Alan Corker, a local amateur painter, called and introduced himself, as did Brian Bull, a mosaicist living in Bristol. They and their wives extended our circle of friends, and social life was better than it had been for a long time.

Alan turned the garage into a studio and began to work again. We started investigating places of local interest, including the Wildfowl Trust at Slimbridge, which we all loved. The children liked the ducks, geese and swans, particularly the Trumpeter swans. Alan and I found the flat area of the Severn Vale, with its wide skies, a new and pleasant environment, and the calm and quiet of the Trust well away from traffic, was a big contrast to the hurly-burly of St. Ives in August. We immediately took out membership of the Trust, and this was a constant source of pleasure for all of us for many years, particularly for Alan and Martin. As always, Alan had his sketchbook with him and did many drawings. The first two paintings he completed after the upheaval of the move were "Ne-ne Goose" and "Goslings", birds at the Wildfowl Trust."

---

44 Pat Dolan used to live near the Lowndes at Halsetown. Valerie described him as 'a spasmodic painter and an architect by training, but not practising. He was a very good looking man with a lovely voice.'

45 Alan Wood was a painter in Cornwall for some years before moving to Cardiff to teach. In the mid seventies he moved again to Canada, where he has stayed and is well known for his large outdoor sculptures.

The family started to attend St. John's village church opposite their house and became friendly with the vicar, Dr. T. A. Ryder, and his wife. He was a historian who had written several books. At the time he was writing 'An account of Cam Church and Parish' and asked Alan to illustrate it for him.

Once settled into their new home physically and with their improvement financially, the Lowndes were able to renew their social life and take the ferry to France to visit the Willetts in Le Thil-Manneville. The Willetts always seemed to have a house full of guests; Nicholas Horsfield was often present. Alan met many famous people at openings of his exhibitions, however he struck up a firm friendship with one of them, the playwright Bill Naughton. Sharing the same Northern working class background, they had a similar outlook on life and enjoyed each other's company. They met as often as possible and kept in touch with letters and phone calls. Bill and his wife Erna were living on the Isle of Man and asked the Lowndes to visit them there. Alan had happy memories of the island from his scouting days, as did Valerie with her own family, so they were very pleased to go. There was much discussion about writing, painting and the theatre.

BACK ROW: (L TO R)

Bill Naughton, Erna Naughton, Valerie Lowndes

FRONT ROW: (L TO R)

Family dog, Mandy Lowndes, Alan Lowndes and Martin Lowndes

Bill Naughton had become really famous with the production of his play 'Alfie' in 1967. The play was a huge success and was made into two films starring Michael Caine and recently, Jude Law. Alfie was the eponymous anti-hero 'who loves, leaves and when he occasionally wrestles with his conscience, he nearly always wins.' Bill was appreciative of Alan's art and often made comments about his paintings. In a letter dated 19th of July, 1976 he wrote, "It's not just that your pictures have a nice lively surface as it were, but there's a lot going on underneath, and each character so varied and distinct. Good old Alan . . . Michael Medwin has one of yours of a coalbagger and definitely has the bag too low down on his back. It could have been that it was slipping, but the balance was skewy. It's worried me a lot."[46] We don't know Alan's reaction to these comments.

Unfortunately the move did not improve Alan's drinking habits. He continued to brew his terrible homemade wine and became a fixture at the Foresters and Railway pubs. Aled Pugh, who lived opposite the Lowndes remembers being hailed by Alan and asked to join him for a drink. Aled found Alan with one of Valerie's stockings hanging up full of a very cloudy liquid with a clothes peg on the end as a sort of tap. Alan was very eager to point out he had discovered this fantastic one day to maturity home brew. Aled found the resultant 'wine' to be absolutely disgusting, but Alan drank it unperturbed. There was a difference between his life in Upper Cam and Cornwall; he did not have quite such violent arguments that had marred some of his time in Cornwall. As Aled said, "Whenever Alan came into the pub, it brought a smile to the lips." He was no longer the out of touch figurative outsider competing against the overwhelming sea of abstract painters.

Though there were no other serious painters immediately round him, he soon made friends with a number of people, particularly Alan Corker an amateur artist and engineer at the local Berkley nuclear power station, who became a boon drinking companion. "Alan (Lowndes) was a very nice person. He always provoked discussion in the local pub. He used to talk a lot about Velazquez, whom he greatly admired, and Alfred Wallis and the eccentricities of Sven Berlin. He pulled no punches and always provoked. I loved going to the Lowndes's Boxing Day parties. People from all over came to those parties." (Alan Corker) Arthur Caddick, a friend, wrote from Nancledra on the 3rd of December, 1972, ". . . I was looking forward to seeing you & was quite grieved at your non-appearance. You may recall . . . the clergyman friend of Dr. Johnson for whom the Dr. conceived a warm liking from the moment this clergyman said, 'I have tried hard to be a philosopher, but cheerfulness keeps breaking in.' This is exactly what happened when you used to call, & I find West Cornwall infinitely duller without you." Alan could be very good company.

Fairly soon after arriving in Upper Cam, he was fortunate to meet and become good friends with Jack Harris F.R.S., a distinguished scientist and scholar, who also loved art and lived in the village of Upper Cam. Jack found Alan to be memorable and brilliant intellectually with a formidable memory. "He was widely read and could quote extensively, he was so bright. Life could be difficult with him: he could cut you down to size in an abrupt way. He was very gregarious and loved snooker. He also had colour television earlier than I did and used it as an excuse to ask me round for alcoholic evenings to watch snooker on T.V." He was very impressed with the way Alan could mix with anyone on equal terms on the grounds, he assumed, that everyone was of the same intellect as himself. Jack found that Alan was painting in his garage, so offered him the old cheese loft in his house as a studio. He was often terrified he would burn the house down with misuse of his gas heater. He also "invited burglars into the house by constantly leaving the door open, when he had finished." However, Jack was not that impressed with Alan's rate of work, he seldom spent more than a couple of hours a day at his easel.

Alan Lowndes always believed that Wally Frost, the landlord of the Railway Inn, Upper Cam, had summed up his paintings as well as anyone, when he said, "He (Alan) is a peculiar sort of painter in that he paints a thing and it is like it in a way and it is not like it at the same time." Alan gave Wally a painting of the pub, which Wally offered for sale after Alan's death. The ceramiscist and Alan's friend, Brian Bull, bought it. On the back of the painting Alan wrote, 'The Railway Inn Cam, June 1972, 15 x 11. For Hazel and Wally Frost'.

---

46 Some other plays by Naughton were: Keep it in the Family 1967, Spring and Port Wine 1964, June Evening 1966, He Was Gone When We Got There 1966 and Derby Day 1994.

Michael Medwin, British actor born 1923 in London, usually seen as a brash young man, cockney crook or a soldier up to all the dodges. He sprinkled these characterisations later with a few lounge-suited wiseacres. He rattled up nearly 70 films before becoming a successful producer.

'THE RAILWAY INN, CAM', *15 x 11 inches, Oil on Board, 1972 (Collection of Brian Bull)*

'DARTS PRACTICE'. *22 x 18 inches Oil on Board, 1971*

'Top Lane'. *18 x 14 inches, Acrylic on Board, 1971 (Collection of Bill Clark)*

'FLOWER IN BOTTLE'. *16.5 x 12.5 inches, Oil on Board, 1972 (Private Collection) Andras Kalman asked Alan to paint a flower piece for his next exhibition. "I'll give him a bloody flower piece," was his riposte, hence the painting above.*

'A Drunk Man', 18 x 22 inches, Oil on Canvas, 1971 (Private Collection)
The painting was sold as 'The Pub Singer' in 1972 by Andras Kalman

Lowndes enjoyed a very successful retrospective exhibition in 1972 organised by the Crane Kalman Gallery in conjunction with the Stockport Art Gallery in 1972. 23rd September - 14th October. David Tomlinson, then a well-known actor and old friend of Andras Kalman opened the exhibition.47 It was a very large exhibition of some 84 paintings covering Alan's career from the forties to 1972 in the splendid exhibition space in the town gallery, which was also filmed by B.B.C. North West as part of a programme discussing the life of Alan Lowndes. Many of the exhibits have already been illustrated. Love Lane Corner and Doss House were 'recent' paintings that were also exhibited.

'Love Lane Corner', 48 x 36 inches, Oil on Canvas, 1970 (Collection of Stockport Art Gallery)

47 David Tomlinson, the son of a solicitor, served for a year in the Grenadier Guards before making his West End debut in 1938. He became famous in the 1960s and starred in over 50 films, including the first Herbie film, The Love Bug, in 1969 and Bedknobs and Broomsticks in 1971. In the early Manchester days, he also managed to steal away one of Kalman's girl friends, but remained good friends.

'OLD DOSS HOUSE'. *30 x 18 inches Oil on Board, 1972 (Private Collection)*

The retrospective exhibition received very flattering comments from the critics.

> *The Darts Match*, the fans of *The Football Match*, the group with their papers of fish and chips in *Love Lane Corner*. They show a keenness of observation and an ability to realise it in paint that would deprecate the label "naive" that has sometimes been attracted to his work.
>
> There is one interesting resemblance to Lowry in that both have relished the contrast afforded to their urban themes by the sea. Lowndes is at his best in the design and colour of *The Land's End* (1970). But in style the work of just on a quarter of a century shows no drastic change. As an autobiographical note relates, he decided to become a painter of pictures at the age of eight or nine and thereafter pursued his objective steadily undeterred by years of penurious living. What Andras Kalman has well summed up as "a sort of aesthetic stamina and a will not to fail", has ample evidence in the present exhibition.

WILLIAM GAUNT.
The Times
27-12-1972

In the Spectator it stated, "Though his work showed considerable awareness of the abstract elements of composition, Alan remained far too interested in people to stop painting them. His great strength was his honesty - always a rare artistic commodity, but rarer still when the main body of his work was produced." Many critics throughout his working life have commented on the 'honesty' of his work, an accolade few artists have received with such regularity. Lowndes would well have appreciated Keats's statement in his Ode on a Grecian Urn, "Beauty is truth, truth beauty".

Lowndes was forthcoming to the press about his painting. He compared his art to the old jazz players, who chose tunes like Tiger Rag and old blues tunes and built upon them the 'equivalent in music of a baroque or Gothic cathedral'. He had painted the North, where he was born and brought up, and just like the jazz players didn't have to think of the individual tunes, he didn't have to think about any particular scene, which left him free to do anything he liked with it. The fact that it was the North was merely incidental, he was painting a time and a feeling and just happened to be there. As he said, "The Midi is a featureless bloody area, but Van Gogh got something out of it. Who the hell has painted anything good in Switzerland with all those beautiful bloody mountains?" He listed his recreations in Who's Who as 'observing the public in public places and public houses'.

Alan also received a letter of congratulations from his old friend Sydney Graham that meant much more to him than the comments of any art critic.

> To see all those things in your book together makes a great thing. I am very much moved by the book Kalman have made. The good timbre of your voice comes out through the collection of your various subjects. I hope you feel pretty good. You should. I am showing it to everybody.
>
> The Cornish Peninsula is green wi' envy.
>
> Love to you all & from Ness. I always said you would turn up trumps. Thanks for the poem-fee.
>
> Love — Sydney

He was very pleased with the success of the Stockport retrospective and for a while gained greatly in self-esteem. The exhibition was not a selling show, but Andras Kalman managed to transfer it to London. As it was too large for the Crane Kalman Gallery, the exhibition was held at the Rutland Gallery, 29 Bruton Street, London. Sales were good. The Lowndes were very pleased, and Andras was delighted that all his efforts had achieved such success. He increased Alan's annual retainer to £3500.00; thus by adding Valerie's salary of £1500.00, the Lowndes had at last a good income for those times. These were heady days for the Lowndes family. Terrance Mullaly wrote in the Daily Telegraph on Wednesday, December 13th, "Alan Lowndes, simply a good artist. If anybody who cares to go to the Rutland Gallery and look closely at the work of Lowndes will learn much about the art of painting."

Alan's feature on Television North West on January 9th, 1973, covered his 1972 Stockport Retrospective and his life in St. Ives and Gloucestershire. He must have been gritting his teeth, when yet again it was suggested that people might consider their children could paint as well as him. As he rightly pointed out, "Everyone tells me they can paint as good as me. All I can say is, let them pack up their job and become a professional painter and have a try at making a living out of it." This reminded him of a comment made by J.B. Priestley, "People always told Priestley that they could write a novel, but 'I haven't got the time'. So he wrote an autobiography, 'I haven't got the time'."

There was a beautiful scene in the film when Alan was walking round the room in the County Hotel, Stockport, viewing and talking about his huge murals. How typical that the council demolished the hotel to enable a supermarket to be built, the new temple of this century. Interestingly he hardly stuttered at all during the filming and interviews.

Programmes for 9 January

BBC1

10.10 Colour
Me? I Just Sing for My Supper
Alan Lowndes, painter
Everyone tells ALAN LOWNDES that if they had the time they, too, could paint the rather direct, strong pictures of the industrial North and the Cornish seascapes that have brought him international recognition.
'Let them have a go – give up their jobs and keep a wife and three kids by painting for a living,' he muses.
This film portrait of the fifth child of a railway clerk follows Alan Lowndes and his philosophy from early garret days in Stockport via a long stay with the artists' colony in St Ives to his present output from a peaceful studio in Cam, Gloucestershire.
Producer BOB MOXLEY
BBC North West

ALAN LOWNDES, UPPER CAM, GLOUCESTERSHIRE, *December 1972. The two paintings propped up are 'Three Seagulls', 1966 and 'Nancledra', 1969 with his Morris Minor tucked in by a house. There is plenty of evidence of his 'demons' in the photograph.*

As a consequence of the success of the 1972 exhibition, Alan and Valerie had the confidence to look for a larger house for their growing family. They found exactly what they wanted at Downside House higher up the hill from the church. It had lovely views. "We could even see the Black Mountains and had an orchard and a lovely garden. We had three reception rooms: Alan had one as a studio. In the large garden he was able to grow potatoes and other vegetables as well. Amanda and Rosalind spent a lot of time at a local riding stable. There were trees for the children to climb, room for us to have friends and family to stay and to give parties, and all seemed set fair for the immediate future."[48]

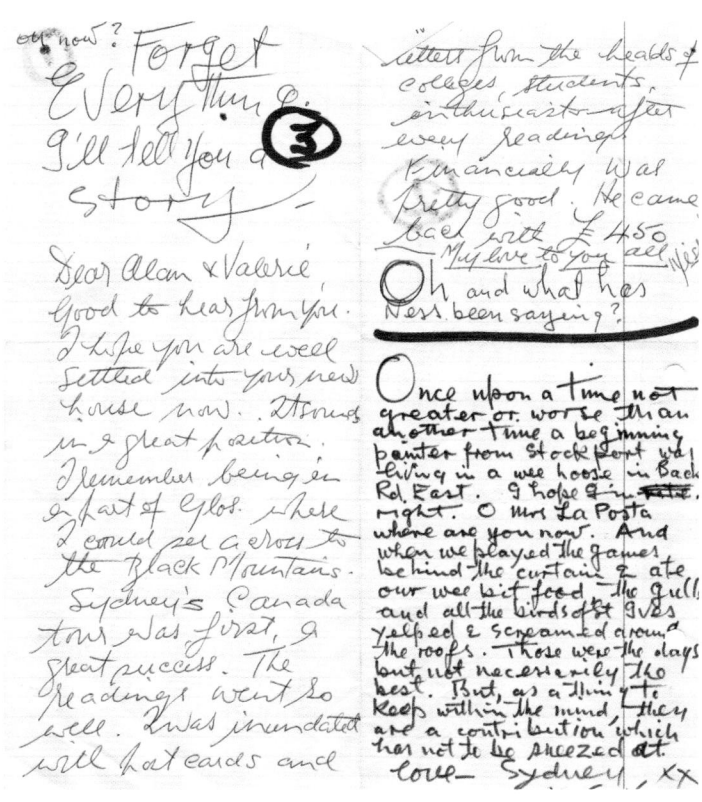

A typical zany welcome from Sydney Graham to their new home (Undated)

48 Valerie Lowndes

Downside House,
Upper Cam,
Gloucestershire,
2004

The family had three good years from 1973 to 1976 in their new home. The children were showing considerable academic ability at school, all three went on to good universities; all became able linguists; Martin was especially brilliant. He wanted to study Latin at A level, but his school was unable to provide a teacher. He decided to teach himself from the beginning and gained an A grade in one year. Martin developed a precocious talent for poetry. He was fortunate to have the assistance of his father's old friend, Sydney Graham. Sydney was a kind man; he made some very objective suggestions to Martin in correspondence over quite a period. Illustrated are letters advising him how to have a poem published in Aquarius, advice not always taken.

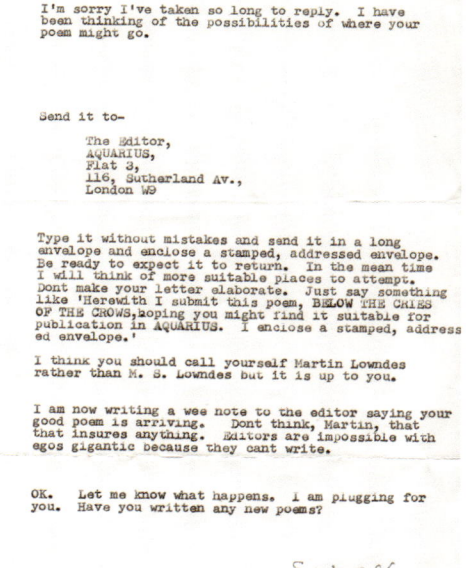
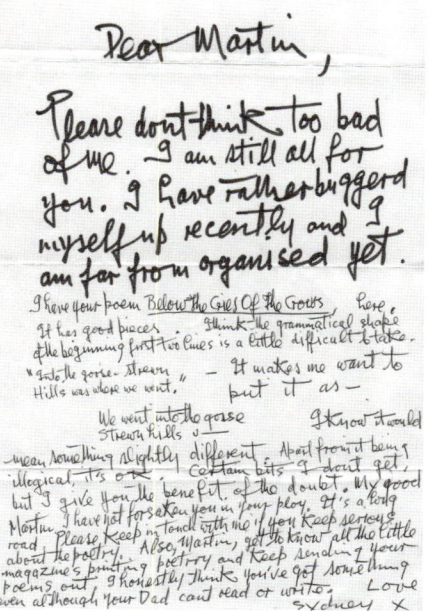

Mandy Lowndes (Centre) *Bell ringing, Cam Church*

Rosalind Lowndes described how her family used to read most of the time. They were always very surprised by the Frost boys when they visited, who wanted to play 'normal' games and kick a football around. Alan was somewhat censorious in some ways: he allowed his children to watch B.B.C. but not I.T.V.. Amusingly, the Lowndes children were thus not allowed to watch Coronation Street, a programme named after one of their father's paintings. Mandy Lowndes always felt he was affectionate and kindly towards his children. Rosalind, on the other hand felt. "He was clearly a hugely articulate man and could reflect on his feelings. He just was never particularly affectionate or warm with me. To me he did not behave like an affectionate father as he was too involved with his painting. He liked small children but seemed to have less tolerance for us as we got older."

However a child of a 'painter' could find life at school not all that straightforward in rural Gloucestershire. Alan was very different to other men; he wasn't in business, wore cravats and was often drunk. Rosalind vividly remembered a child saying to her, "Your dad's an artist?" "Yes". "You mean a piss artist." Fortunately in a way, a combination of their father's ambitions and such events at school made all three of them all the more determined to succeed. Rosalind commented, "My father wanted Mandy to be a musician, Martin to be the brightest and me to be an actress . . . It was his idea that all his children should go into the arts, but none into painting . . . We were never encouraged to do that . . . He wanted us to be properly clever, but I think he forgot in the middle of all that sometimes to let us be children. We were all very self motivated, we just did it, we were never nagged to work."

Rosalind tells a story about the occasion she hurt herself at school and was brought home by the headmaster. When they knocked on the door, Alan was upstairs. He tried to come down to let them in, but tumbled all the way down and hurt himself. The Headmaster had to put Alan to bed, which was somewhat embarrassing.

Lowndes did indeed have strong feelings for his family, even though his behaviour was normally somewhat self-centred. In his letter to Elizabeth Boston (Horsfield/Cilli), September 27th, 1977 he wrote, "I will have to bring up the old law about the sake of the children, but it is for their sake. I love Valerie . . . My life and times has been mostly spent in the middle of broken marriages and one parent families. The looks on the faces of the children nearly destroy me. Only recently I realised I was deprived and was brought up in a one parent family, but a mother dying isn't the same as a divorce. I'm still not sophisticated enough. This cheery meeting of Ex's and first name terms of various adults and children - not for me - a dark brooding half Celt Northerner."

In 1973 he was asked by the Curwen Press to paint some images for prints, which were duly published. In a later letter to Andras Kalman he said of this experience, "In between these (two large paintings) I recently completed 14 plates for the two lithographs - not to mention two painted designs for the lithographs."

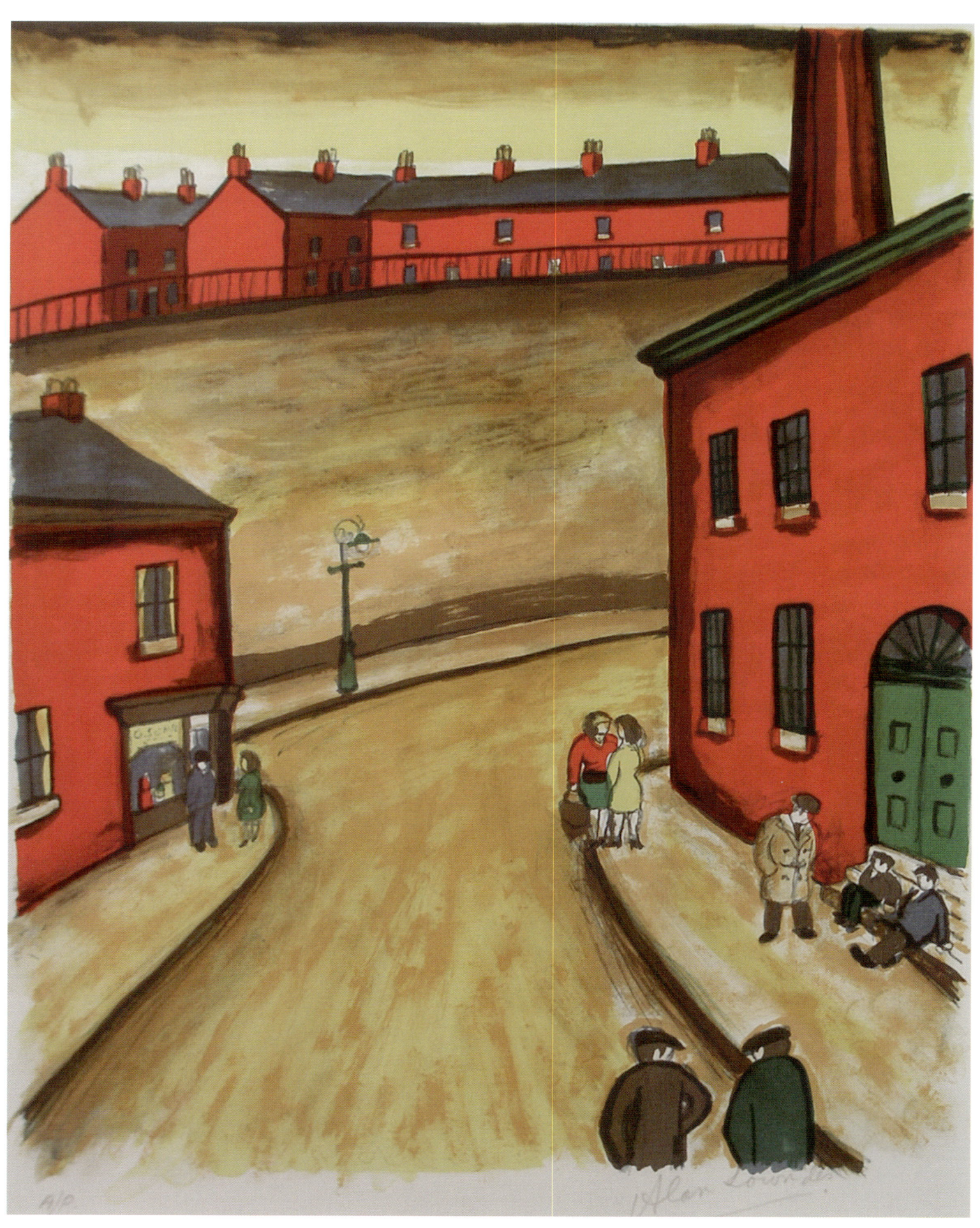

'STOCKPORT'. *19.5 x 16.5 inches, 1973. Lithograph by The Curwen Press on Five Plates*

'THE PAWN BROKER.' 19.5 x 16.5 inches, 1975, Lithograph by The Curwen Press on Five Plates. This print is very similar to 'The Pawn Shop' painted in 1955.

On May 1st, 1972 Alan received a letter from Dr. Gibbs stating "I noticed you had a picture of Cardiff, which in fact had been sold. I am writing to know whether you would be prepared to accept a Commission to make three pictures in Cardiff; my two grandfathers were associated with Cardiff in the days of its early expansion, and I would like recorded the office of one in Mount Stuart Square, The Docks, Cardiff, and the home of the other - also in the dock area - and possibly the view from the office over the Cardiff Docks and Penarth Head." Alan wrote back to him saying he had only made brief visits so far to the city and a few sketches done whilst he was in the city to lecture at Cardiff Art College. (No doubt arranged by Pat Dolan, who was teaching at the college.) He was very taken by Cardiff and readily agreed to undertake the commission.

Over a period of several months a meeting was arranged with Dr. Gibbs and terms agreed for the commission. Lowndes wrote to Dr. Gibbs in an undated letter in 1973 saying that the terms of the commission were ideal, but "Would it be possible for you to let us have £500.00 pretty soon?" He complained that the Kalman Gallery was particularly slow in paying after exhibitions, "The Americans would call it the Pied Piper syndrome. All you did was pipe a tune - or paint a few pictures - whilst I have all the worries of big business, big profits, not to mention big ego etc. . . ." He then continued with some interesting comments about his painting. "Whilst doing the drawing for the office, I saw about ten possibilities from where I stood sketching. Years ago in Stockport, I did literally dozens of paintings from almost the same spot on one street corner, and I got the same feeling again. What I want now (and I am sure I will get it) is some good, dull, overcast days - I never was a fine day, blue sky, painter - or hardly ever."

There then followed several letters explaining why the project had to be delayed; he had to do some lithographs for the Curwen Press and he had to go to hospital to have a quinsy removed. "Alan did have a quinsy. I'd forgotten all about it. It is as you say in the throat, either an inflammation, a swelling or even a lump. In this case it needed either lancing or removing, I can't remember which. Alan told us when he came home that the doctor had said, just before starting this treatment 'This is the first time I've done this'. Not exactly reassuring words for a patient awaiting a delicate operation. But as quinsy is a pretty rare condition, this was probably forgiveable. Anyway Alan recovered all right, there were no further problems with that."[49] Lowndes then had the Stockport Retrospective and the B.B.C. film to take up his time and various 'side issues' as he described them to Dr. Gibbs. He was still short of money and suggested to Dr. Gibbs that he should visit him at Bloomfield House and purchase some pictures in a letter dated May 13th. All went well and a purchase was made. The Doctor and his family felt somewhat embarrassed to be taking pictures from his wall, whereas Alan was delighted to be selling. Soon afterwards Alan completed his commission and received a further cheque for £500.00.

Lowndes became very interested in Tiger Bay, the docks area of Cardiff, during his visit to Pat Dolan. "There were the docks and the streets of small houses, then the posher houses that belonged to the owners and sea captains and everybody was around in the same area. How much better planned was all this than today. They weren't wonderful houses, but everybody knew everybody, there were shops and pubs, and now they are putting up blocks of flats which aren't very good architecturally anyway."

Further good news, Dr. Gibbs wrote to Alan on June 15th, 1973 saying that he was the Buyer for the Contemporary Art Society of Wales and was especially interested in any other of Alan's works that had a Cardiff setting. The Society bought 'Street Scene Cardiff Docks, 24 x 20 inches, Oil on Board, 1974' (Illustrated on Page 201) with the persuasive Dr. Gibbs writing in the Society's A.G.M. Report, ". . . Naïve? Innocent? Child-Like? But there is nothing innocent or child-like about Alan Lowndes's observation. He has a most experienced eye. He painted hard and full time and scorned to teach to give himself a secure income. He painted some ten pictures in Cardiff, nearly all of Bute Town now demolished and the subject matter of this picture gives it an added importance for our collection."

'SHIPS STORES MERCHANT, TIGER BAY, CARDIFF', *30 x 20 inches, Oil on Canvas, 1973 (Private Collection)*

'LOUISA STREET, TIGER BAY, CARDIFF', *16 x 20 inches, Oil on Canvas, 1973*

'Eleanor Street, Tiger Bay, Cardiff', 20 x 36 inches, Oil on Canvas, 1973

Pages Over (198-199): 'Stuart Street, Cardiff', 20 x 30 inches, Oil on Canvas, 1973
(Collection of the Crane Kalman Gallery)

Penguin Books selected Alan's 'Street Scene, Cardiff Docks', to illustrate the cover of 'There Was a Young Man from Cardiff' by Dannie Abse, an amusing and moving autobiography of his early life in Cardiff.[50]

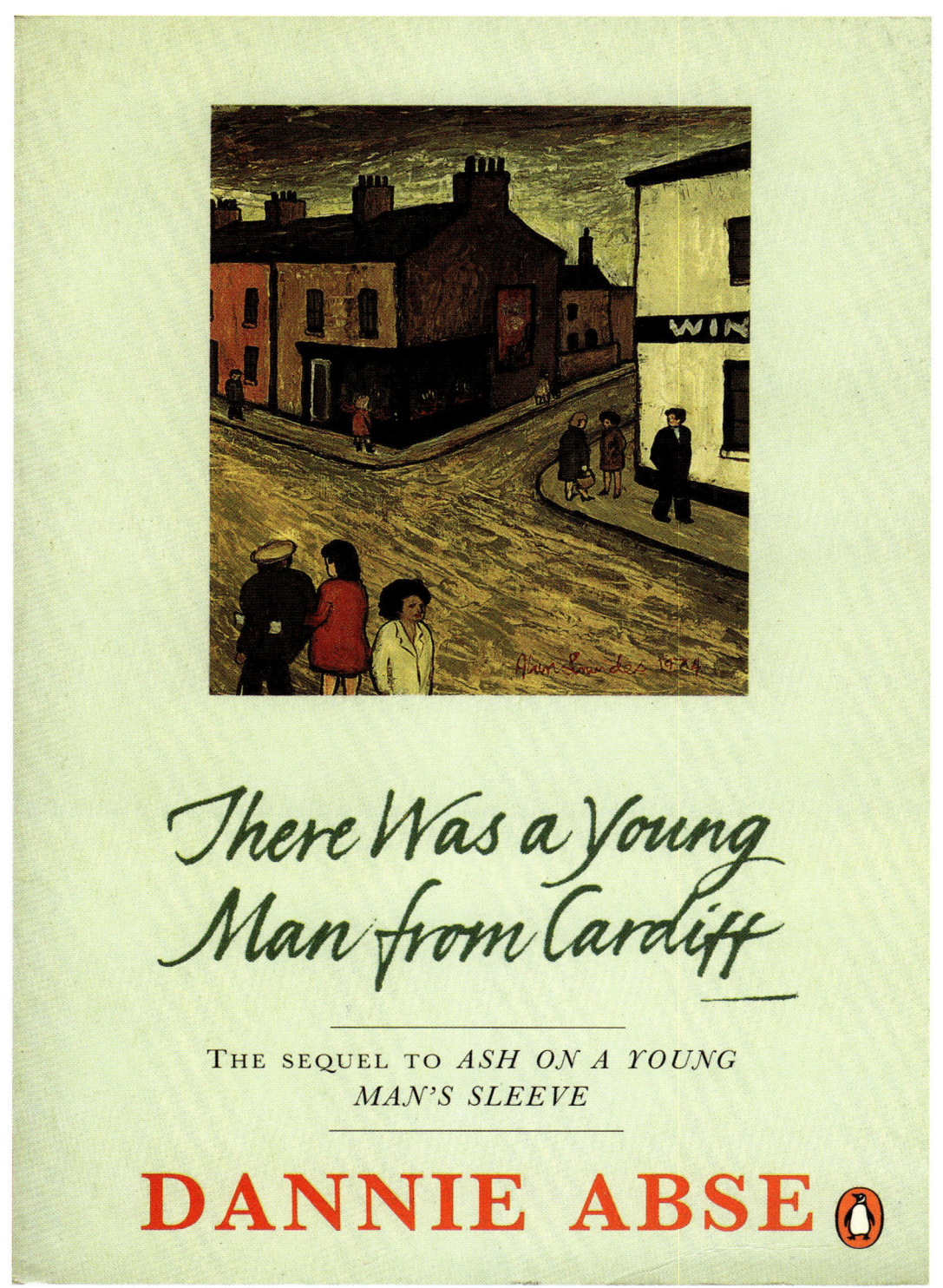

50 There Was a Young Man from Cardiff was published by Penguin Books in 1992. ISBN number 13579108642 and suitably printed by Clays Ltd. of St. Ives.

RIGHT PAGE (201):
DETAIL OF 'CARDIFF STREET SCENE', 24 x 20 inches, Oil on Board, 1974 (Collection of the Contemporary Art Society of Wales, currently loaned to Clwyd Fine Arts Trust)

'THE KICK OFF'. 30 x 40 inches, Oil on Canvas, 1970. Title later changed in 1972 to 'The Football Match'. The positioning of the players would suggest that Lowndes was not very knowledgeable about football. (Collection of James Huntington-Whitely)

On February 8th, 1974, Alan received a letter from Meriel Larken representing the Goaldiggers Trust in which she thanked Alan for allowing him to use one of his paintings for a book cover. "You kindly allowed Willis Hall and Michel Parkinson to use your painting - The Football Match - as the cover for their anthology of football - "Football Report". Please will you let me know if you did not get a copy so that I can post one off to you without delay." Considering Alan took little interest in sport, the use of his painting for the cover was flattering indeed. There was some earlier correspondence between the Lowndes and the publishers about payment for copyright. Naturally, Valerie felt Alan deserved a small fee for the use of his picture. Andras Kalman persuaded him to forget about money, the publicity was worth more than a small payment. His logic was right, but Alan, as ever, needed money in the short term. On the bright side, all royalties went to the Goaldiggers Trust.

'FOOTBALL REPORT', EDITED BY WILLIS HALL AND MICHAEL PARKINSON. *Published by Pelham Books Ltd., ISBN No. 0 7207 0724 2. The painting depicted on the cover was entitled 'THE KICK OFF', and was changed in 1972 to 'THE FOOTBALL MATCH', 30 x40 inches, Oil on Canvas, 1970. The trust had been set up by Parkinson and Hall to help improve facilities to enable youngsters to play football.*

Alan had a notorious reputation for his driving skills. Jack Harris vividly described Alan's appalling driving in his superb article in the Guardian, 26th of May, 1984. "It was his driving that made him most notorious with the locals. He had a unique technique. He would sit in the car ever so slowly getting the car to maximum revs before letting in the clutch quite rapidly. The result was a series of lurches or hops along the road, rather like the movement of a kangaroo. Quite frequently he hit things - walls, gates, houses, other cars. One night he hit the pub. He never injured himself nor anyone else, by some miracle. The funniest sight was the panic on the faces of pub customers . . . when news got round that Alan was outside trying to get into the car park. He claimed one night after he had stalled the car three times crossing the busy A38, it was the nervousness of his passengers, which when transmitted to him, made him make mistakes. Nothing would shake him from his conviction that it was his passengers who were at fault. It was no use pointing out that he used to hit things when driving alone."

Brian Bull told of his organisational abilities. Alan asked him if he could drive him to his forthcoming exhibition in Farnborough (New Ashgate Gallery, Farnham, 6 - 29 April 1976). He gave him strict instructions to be at his house at 8 a.m. precisely. Brian duly arrived at the appointed place and time to discover Alan clutching a detailed itinerary for the journey. Once under way, the itinerary turned out to the exact times he wanted to call in at various pubs en route. To Brian's utter amazement they arrived at the gallery in time for the opening and free wine. Lowndes had a similar itinerary for the return trip.

Unfortunately the good days were coming to an end. Alan's drinking and rowing had its effects on the family in general. Rosalind Lowndes commented: "Probably my fondest memories of my Dad are when we were with people like the Frosts, they brought a level of camaraderie and light-heartedness to our household as they were so boisterous and such fun. There were five big sons and they were energetic. I suppose we were more shy and could appear bookish. They were my favourite times with the family though. We had a fantastic holiday with them in Andouse, because Terry is a family man. I loved it when we were with them, but then we'd go to see Sydney. They just got absolutely blind drunk and then they'd get senseless drunk. I remember one year going to Cornwall to see Roger Hilton, who was sitting on his bed very ill, drinking. We drank with him and then we went on to see Sydney. They fell out, like they always fell out . . . and then he and Sydney would fight, it was childish really. I used to find it exhausting. I remember Sydney locking my dad in the cupboard under our stairs."[51]

The more dependent and affected by alcohol, the more depressed and critical he became. He had a massive chip on his shoulder about abstract painting, especially as a consequence of living in Cornwall. He tended to become rather defensive and angry the minute anything went wrong. He never felt he had gained the recognition he deserved. Alan always took the chance to view galleries, but he did not go to them to tout for business. "He wasn't like Terry, he saw it as prostitution to do like Heron and Frost and all that lot that did. He couldn't be a publicist, so he had a rather Sixties romantic view that if your art was good, the world would come to him. I think he was a little intimidated by someone like Patrick Heron and Terry, who were wily and very clever . . . He didn't have the confidence to move in those worlds . . . He didn't find that niche for himself. I always felt he was probably someone who didn't belong anywhere."[52] Alan was certainly no 'Sillery for ever plotting behind the arras'.[53]

Rosalind has touched upon Alan's basic insecurity, which was also commented on by the painter Karl Weschke. Slim Ingram felt that Alan was born out of his time. If he had been a young man in the sixties, he would have been much more part of the scene and would have been wanted and seen to be wanted. He was undoubtedly dependent on his long relationship with Andras Kalman, whatever he might have said about him to others; it enabled him to avoid 'touting for business'. Alas his world was about to change fundamentally.

Lowndes had always held deep mistrust of paper qualifications. In Cornwall, living amongst many other artists, he was sheltered from the growing tendency in the world to recognise and demand qualifications. He quoted Aldous Huxley, "In the old days architects

---

51 and 52 Rosalind Lowndes
53 Sillery was a wily don featuring in a number of Anthony Powell's great series of novels, 'A Dance to the Music of Time'.

only built palaces and cathedrals and the ordinary man built his own house. In Cornwall we lived in a house, which was 250 years old and had never seen an architect, yet it looked well on its site - it fitted in visually. Today all these highly trained people get the drawing board out - these are the people who are always bleating about the environment - yet they cannot build a pleasant village, not even one like this (Upper Cam), and this isn't an extraordinary one. Modern architecture is self-conscious, artificial and inefficient." He certainly has a point, which is perhaps even more relevant today as 'paper qualifications' mean less and less. Nevertheless his lack of any training of any sort, except as a decorator, did increase his growing insecurity.

The quantity of his work was becoming variable. He was also creating greater and greater difficulties for Valerie with a mounting spiral of debts. It happened that Nicholas Horsfield was visiting the Lowndes, when they received a letter from Andras Kalman on May 13th, 1975. He was no longer going to pay them a stipend. The news was a bombshell for the Lowndes family; it was a total nightmare scenario in the financial mire in which they had found themselves. Andras felt guilty to the end of his life about the letter, but what else could he have done? For years Alan's work and attitude had been far too irregular as a consequence of his love affair with alcohol. Years of over indulgence in alcohol had their tale to tell.

His own words tell the story, "The finances got worse, debts bigger. Kalman explained that due to selling my work for bigger prices - by some financial logic known only to him, he had to pay me less for my paintings. I could do nothing. I was impossible and drunk most of the time. Eventually I couldn't eat at all and developed a pain in my stomach. Every drink I drank was like swallowing red hot razor blades and I couldn't stop drinking."

'A Memorial tree', 20 x 30 inches, Oil on Canvas, 1976 (Private Collection)

Chapter 11 - Catastrophe, Illness, Happiness and Finale

The final catastrophe was totally predictable. There had been a volume of correspondence between Alan and Andras discussing their individual problems. Andras had become more and more frustrated with their long-standing arrangement, whereby he had to take whatever Alan sent him. He had less and less choice to make for his customers, especially as Alan's output declined even further. Alan wrote to Andras on March 11th, 1975 responding to a letter that had urged him to think of his family and reputation, stop drinking so much, stop using photographs and do some work. Alan's letter was somewhat combative and made excuses for his lack of work, though quite mild considering the likely consequences of Kalman's decision. Throughout the many letters over the years between Alan and Andras, Alan always seems to adopt quite a subservient stance.

Amongst other comments he stated, ". . . I did take time out for Roger Hilton's funeral in Cornwall and to pay my respects to Bryan Wynter, who died a few days previously. Both were old friends of long standing.[54] My only 'social' visit to the North was to my brother's funeral last year. I drew a small painting from that. Not very happy occasions ... No painter I have ever met has taken much notice of advice or instructions from non painters. I am no exception."

Andras wrote across his letter, 'Banker's Orders. I will buy no more.' Valerie wrote a long and reasoned letter amongst other matters pointing out, "You feel that Alan is not sending up enough work to cover the £3500.00 you pay annually ... As we have no idea what the current prices of his paintings are, it is difficult to be realistic about how many paintings are worth £3500.00."

Andras wrote back on May 12th, 1975 offering "to buy £3,000 – £3,500 worth of paintings from you each year, but I will buy only what I like. You paint what you like, but I will only take what I like." He then went on to say he was returning some of Alan's paintings and offered him an exhibition, but as times were hard, it was not possible to give a date. He concluded, "... but as from the 1st of June I will not pay any more banker's orders until we have caught up with each other as far as my advances go." On May 13th he wrote, "Further to our telephone conversation of this morning, I now write to confirm the following.

From October 1st 1976 all banker's orders payable to you will cease.

By that date I want to have enough pictures to come level with the money I have advanced to you . . . Then from the 1st of October onwards you will bring pictures up to London when they are ready, and I will buy those I want and pay for them . . ."

Alan wrote on the same day apologising to Andras for sounding angry and fatuous. He commented that he did use photographs in his work, but only for reference. Valerie had earlier pointed out to Andras in her letter that Alan had hundreds of drawings. He begged Andras not to cancel his banker's order and to have regard for his family. Alan agreed he had not supplied enough paintings that year, but three were on their way to him. He had been depressed, but was now hard at work on two paintings forty-eight inches wide by thirty-six inches high entitled 'The Threepenny Rush' and 'Castle Market'.

On March 2nd 1976 Andras wrote to Alan enclosing a price list for his promised exhibition. He outlined to Alan exactly how a sale of a picture worked financially and who received what. He was pleased with the show, it was going well. He added one realistic statement, "More tough writing on the wall is that if you put your pictures into auction, whether Sotheby's or not, without a gallery you find they do not sell." Sadly, the Lowndes were to discover how true this was, when they later tried to sell paintings at auction or other galleries. On the next page part of an exhibition of the work of northern painters organised by Peter Davies at the Pelter Sands Gallery in November, 1989 to promote his book, The Northern School, is illustrated, together with a letter from the gallery confirming sales of only three drawings by Lowndes. How the situation has changed today.

---

54 Terry Frost told Leon Suddaby, an art dealer, an amusing tale about what occurred at the funeral. Terry and Alan decided to give Roger a fitting oblation by pouring a bottle of whisky over his coffin in recognition of all the alcohol he had consumed in his lifetime. At the right moment, Terry unscrewed the half bottle he had brought with them and was about to pour it over the recumbent and deceased Roger. Alan grabbed the bottle, swigged all the whisky and threw the empty bottle onto the coffin. 'What a pity to waste good whisky' was Alan's comment.

```
Tuesday 28th November 1989

Re: A Northern School Exhibition

                                                    £
3 pictures sold as per attatched list,
less Pelter/Sands commission:

Less ½ share of expenses as follows:

Printing of brochures & invitations         815.00
Wine at preview                              87.50
Commissionaire                                9.50
Postage                                      63.50
Total                                       975.50
÷ 28 exhibitors                              34.83

Balance, cheque enclosed
```

		£	Kindly lent by
1	W.S. Graham (Portrait)	N.F.S.	
2	Françoise (Portrait)	500	
3	Beach Scene	800	
4	Musical Clowns	N.F.S.	
5	Painter & Critics		Dr. J.E. Harris
6	Darts Player		"
7	Band Practice		"
8	Logan Rock, Cornwall	400	
9	Lighthouse, Ibiza	N.F.S.	
10	The Accordian Player	500	
11	Market Place, Tetbury	N.F.S.	
12	Cottage near Slimbridge	400	
13	Flower & Baby Ros.	N.F.S.	
14	Amanda & Martin	N.F.S.	
15	Valerie	N.F.S.	
16	Tarted-up Pub	500	
17	Pig & Chicken	700	
18	Self Portrait 1964	N.F.S.	

		£	Kindly lent by
19	Nude & Figtree	N.F.S.	
20	View from the Window	N.F.S.	
21	Valerie, Mandy & Martin	N.F.S.	
22	Self Portrait 1953	N.F.S.	
23	Cat	N.F.S.	
24	Gloucester Barge	500	
25	Love & the Bandit	450	
26	Mandy & Martin		Miss M. Scarr
27	Pheasants	400	
28	Drifter		Mr. L. Holmes
29	Tourette sur Loup		"
30	Cottage in Mousehole		Mr. A. Breach
31	Zennor Church		Mrs. J. Hawkins
32	Girl & Bear		Mrs. W. Holcombe
33	Newlyn Lighthouse		"
34	Cat Confrontation		Mr. & Mrs. W. Frost
35	Railway Inn		"
36	Bert		Mrs. E. Gemmill

PAGE RIGHT: *A delightful article by the great comic actor, Peter Bowles, in which he describes his purchase of 'GIRL UNDRESSING', 9 x 6 inches, Acrylic on Board, 1967, in the 'Over 21' Magazine, March 1981, and states his fulsome appreciation of Lowndes's paintings - pleasant praise at a difficult time for the family.*

"...but I know what I like"

Peter Bowles talks to Mary Davis Peters about Alan Lowndes' 'Girl Dressing'

Peter Bowles is a brilliantly versatile, totally professional actor. Also a very nice person, who refuses to play the Star, because he hasn't, he firmly points out, been one for all that long. He's possibly most widely known for his definitive brash-but-lovable parvenu in To the Manor Born, *but has a long and solid list of films and West End plays, as well as television successes behind him — and something really juicy coming up;* Mr Bultitude *in the television version of Anstey's delicious Victorian classic comedy,* Vice-Versa. *Peter grew up in the Midlands, won a scholarship to R.A.D.A., which can't have been easy in a year that included Finney, O'Toole, Alan Bates and Richard Briers. After which he was told (by an agent who, says Peter, "was a prophet") that he wouldn't make it till he was 40. He's obviously happily married to a charming ex-actress, Susan Bennett; they have three teenage children; also Bob, a huge, hearthrug-style dog ("only half Old English sheepdog"). Lives in a sunny, picture-filled house near the Thames; says that his only hobby is looking at paintings, to which he reacts so directly that "It does more for my circulation than jogging".*

Girl Dressing
Alan Lowndes (1921-1978)

❝If you haven't seen many of Alan Lowndes' paintings — just a few north-country town scenes, perhaps — you might think of him as 'School of Lowry' — I did, until I saw about 30 of his paintings grouped together. Landscapes with and without figures; seascapes, figure studies, all painted with such a marvellous 'smack you in the eyes' directness that it was quite clear that he wasn't School of anyone. He was very much his own man. Though he was, of course, a great friend and admirer of Lowry, who encouraged him to become a professional painter, instead of a professional painter-and-decorator, which is what he was — almost all the 'training' he ever had. "Just put it down as good as you can, then leave it" was the great Lowry's advice, which surely holds good for any form of art, not only for painting.

Painting of this kind is easy to appreciate because it's uncluttered by 'technique'; you know — and I expect Lowndes knew — that the mirror-image isn't correct in relation to the actual figure. But it means that we see more of that beautiful body; a lot more worth having than painstaking art-school 'accuracy'.

One reason why I'm attracted to this painting is that it fills up a gap in my experience, my knowledge — let me explain. The girl looks about 16 or 17, alone in her bedroom. Well, when I was 16 and 17, I was alone in *my* bedroom too, wondering what girls of my age were doing in *their* rooms. Now, thanks to Alan Lowndes, I know.

I also like this painting and, in fact, bought it, because it has great tenderness. The girl looks so vulnerable, standing there in that chilly, depressing room, but Lowndes has caught and shown us the total beauty and femininity of woman, with glamorous adornment deliberately cut to the minimum — just mirror, brush, talc and deodorant. She's got nothing — except hope. I'd like to put my arms round her, very gently, and offer her all the things she wants out of life. But that bright blue bra suggests spirit — so I'd probably get a clip round the ear if I tried.

After I'd bought the painting, I discovered that Lowndes is admired — and collected — by many actors. It doesn't surprise me. Acting has to do with getting to the truth; to the essence of a character or situation, and communicating it as clearly and as simply as possible. Horrendously difficult. Alan Lowndes does this superbly well; no wonder actors recognise and enjoy his artless technique. Funny — I didn't use that expression deliberately, but I realise that it's particularly significant in this context.

A lot of people are fooled by Art with a capital A — just as they're fooled by Acting with a capital A. But in fact, the smaller the 'a' the better; don't blur the message; don't give anyone the excuse to talk about the way the paint — or whatever — is used, on canvas or on stage 'in relationship to time and space'. Just let the subject speak absolutely directly, like the girl in the picture — totally uncluttered and unadorned.

There's a haunting nostalgia about some of Lowndes' work — it somehow shows you how things were *as you remember them;* never mind how they really were. The only real truth is what's in your own memory. And as I was brought up in Nottingham, in an environment not unlike Lowndes', many of his pictures do recall memories — or, as in the case of *Girl Dressing,* even remembered imaginings. Surely a painter who can do that has a touch of greatness.❞

Andras had looked after Alan very well indeed, considering everything. It is the sad truth with alcoholics that the demon drink becomes the centre of their world taking over from everything and everyone else. The effect on alcoholics' families is usually predictable, especially the demands made on the spouse. Valerie was no different. She had an increasingly difficult time as Alan became worse. He was continually depressed and critical of all and sundry, jumping from euphoria to self-pity. He was constantly disparaging other artists' work, including Terry Frost, whom he liked very much as a person. He was more critical of the 'fashionable abstract artists', who received so much acclaim. He was bitter and twisted with Valerie; she was just a middle class woman wanting middle class things etc.. It is impossible for people close to an alcoholic to appreciate they no longer matter compared with their 'God', alcohol.

A friend and gallery owner wrote him am amazingly frank and kind letter of encouragement to persuade Alan to give up alcohol. He discussed paintings he had in stock and his admiration for Alan's work, he then wrote, "The third reason I write to you, and dare to do so at all, is that I am an alcoholic and it would be stupid of me to pretend that I did not know that you (at least) suffer from a similar demon. For demon it is, and the only totally SELFISH thing that I have ever done, in 1962 on the last occasion, was to give it up. For all the unselfish reasons, like life and work and wife and family and Christ on the cross - not to mention all the bank managers in every cupboard - are less than sufficient to give people like you and I any pause longer than a few days. Be as selfish as I was lucky enough to be selfish fourteen years ago and you may become as happy as I am now. I pray that this might be so for you." Alas the advice was not heeded. Alan was too dependent on alcohol and his alter ego life in the pub.

Excessive alcohol degrades the body, which can clearly be seen in Alan's case from the two photographs above; the first on the left was taken in his studio in the mid seventies, the second on the right was taken in St. Ives in 1964 for the cover of the Osborne Gallery exhibition. Nevertheless he was still painting some very good pictures however much alcohol he may have consumed.

'Pont Neuf, Dieppe', 24 x 20 inches, Oil on Canvas, 1974 (Collection of Stephen Gould)

'The Market House', 24 x 27 inches, Oil on Board, 1973 (Collection of the Crane Kalman Gallery)

'CHATTING ON THE DOORSTEP', 20 x 11 inches, Oil on Card, 1963 (Collection of the Crane Kalman Gallery)

PAGE LEFT (214): DETAIL OF 'THE RECTORY FARM, SLIMBRIDGE'. *22 x 18 inches, Oil on Canvas, 1977 (Collection of Stephen Gould)*

'THE DARTS PLAYERS'. *18 x 26 inches, Oil on Canvas, 1976*

Left Page (216):
Detail of 'At Band Practice'.
30 x 20 inches, Oil on Board, 1974

'Two Friends Meeting', 22 x 20 inches, Oil on Board, 1976

'A Clean Sweep', *18 x 14 inches, Oil on Board, 1976 (Private Collection)*

'Brace Girdles Count'. 20 x 16 inches, Gouache, 1976

'HILL IN SNOW', 24 x 26 inches, Oil on Board, 1977 (Collection of Bill Clark)

PAGE RIGHT (221): DETAIL OF 'NO THROUGH ROAD', 20 x 16 inches, Oil on Board, 1974 (Private Collection)

By 1977 the debt situation had become very serious indeed for the family. Their very supportive bank manager and his wife had come to their house for a social visit. He commented to Valerie, "You should never worry about money. Married to someone who can take a blank sheet of paper or canvas and turn it into something beautiful, a work of art, you will never be short of money." "If only!" Valerie thought. Alan of course knew better. 'The further from the easel, the more money to be made out of art' being one of his sayings. Unfortunately the sympathetic bank manger was promoted to a London branch, his successor was horrified at their enormous overdraft and demanded immediate repayment. The Lowndes were told to sell their big house. Alan refused to be part of this; he even told prospective buyers that the house was not for sale. Events were about to overtake him in a very serious way.

His health was severely under threat. Brian Bull attested to Alan's poor appetite. He always had very poor teeth, which made eating difficult: "He would sit at meals playing with his food, except for French onion soup." Heavy smoking over the years did not help his health. Excessive alcohol on its own is bad enough, but combined with heavy smoking and not eating, the effect on the human body is extreme indeed. Physically alcoholism was attacking him seriously; his stomach started to swell with the growing effect of alcoholism, which retains water in the system resulting in weight gain and bloating. He spent a considerable portion of the day sleeping and finally he suffered from liquid forming behind his eyes (Corneal Aedema), and his sight became blurred. His heavy smoking over many years also caused nicotine to damage his retina. It is well known that alcoholism damages the liver and brain, but it also damages the heart by changing the structure and functioning of the heart cells. There is also a degree of malnutrition, as alcoholics need less food and hence create a change in the biochemistry of the body. Alan had never eaten properly throughout his life.

In early 1977, after protesting for some time that he did not need to see a doctor, he finally had became so seriously ill he had to see his G.P.. The doctor was horrified at how ill he was and immediately sent him to hospital. Not surprisingly cirrhosis of the liver was diagnosed. "A seriously ill husband, children to provide for and bills to pay spelt a looming crisis. That first evening I persuaded Martin to empty his money box and lend me enough money to buy petrol to visit Alan in hospital. Next day, in desperation, I phoned Andras as a friend rather than a dealer, and he kindly sent me enough money to get me through the next week or two. Brian Bull took some paintings and tried to sell them, but wasn't very successful. Soon after this I received a letter from the Artists' General Benevolent Institution reminding me that our annual contribution was due. I replied that we couldn't send anything this year because of our problems, which I outlined. By return of post came a most welcome letter telling me to send the unpaid bills and discuss further help, which they gave. This enabled us to survive for the next few weeks, until the house sale went through.

The medical staff was not too optimistic about Alan's future. The doctors managed to remove the main causes of his bloated stomach and liquid behind the eyes. They told him he was not going to see old bones and would not live at all, if he continued to drink. He had a volume of letters from his old friends and poems from Sydney.

12-10-77   "Now that you have stopped drinking and I have stopped shagging we should become quite rich and respectable." Pat Dolan

07-10-77   "Jane and myself are very sorry to hear that you are in hospital and we hope you are now feeling better and responding to treatment. One thing you will have to take it easy and go on the wagon and be very careful with the hard stuff." Tony O'Malley

29-11-77   "You're getting right skinny with your news. I haven't heard from you since away in June. Are you still on the wagon or wagonette?" Bill Naughton

RIGHT: A TYPICAL
ZANY CARD FROM
SYDNEY GRAHAM
TO CHEER UP THE
FAMILY

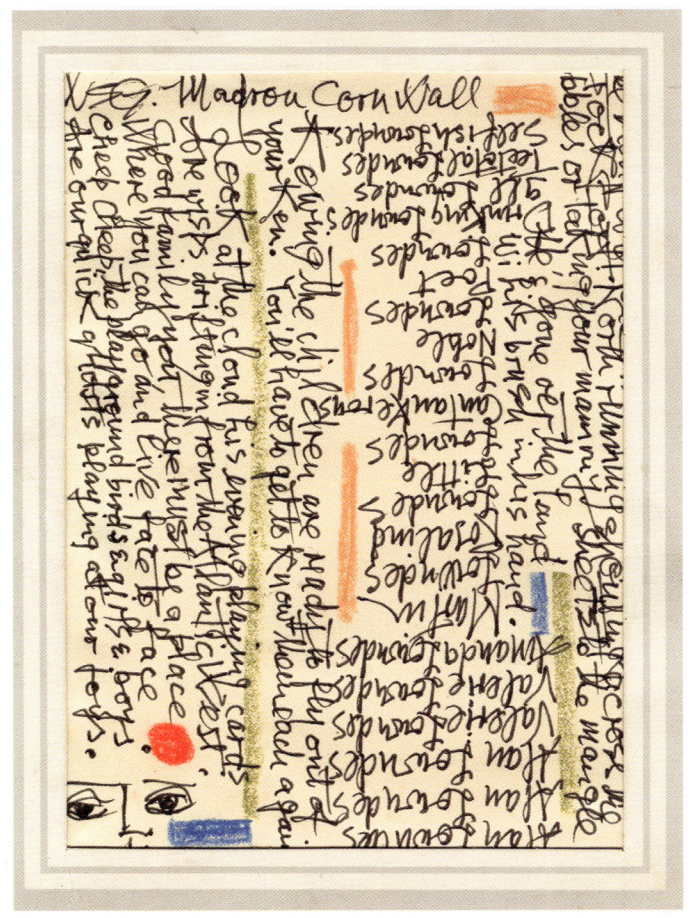

4, Mountview Cottages, Madron, Penzance, Cornwall, England.

BAD GOOD BOY ALAN,

Of course I did not bring you up in bread street or
fish street or whatever the street was called. You
gave me great shooses of something. There we were
going through our lives not quite knowing if we were
going to make anything.

In a kind of way I know you, Alan. You are a tough boyo.
You are a boy of the streets of Stockport. Maybe just
now you are going through a bit difficult to take.

MY DEAR MY DEAR easy-to-fall-out-with man, your
Stockport heart and all you represent as a man from
your work, will make you angry and come up through this
quickly and be as bad and good as ever you were.

This is a letter to you saying- Come the Boy. How
Can I do better? Keep all your courage no matter in what
form it is couched. In a good mood I love you.

You are my heart's delight,
Sydney X

A RATHER POIGNANT POEM FROM SYDNEY GRAHAM TO ALAN LOWNDES TO WISH HIM WELL

'THE YELLOW CHAIR'. *14 x 10 inches, Oil on Canvas, 1977 (Private Collection) This was the last painting Lowndes completed before succumbing to his first illness in 1977.*

Alan was very shocked, and on his release from hospital, made great efforts to stop drinking alcohol. Valerie had prepared a bed for him downstairs, remembering Roger Hilton's long spell in a downstairs room when he was ill. Alan insisted on finding the strength to go upstairs: he was determined to get better. "He became more like the man I had married: good company, even-tempered, almost grateful to me for sorting out the money problems. Eventually in June 1977, the house sale was completed and we were able to move into 13 St. George's Road, a small semi nearer to work and to school. It was a bit hard on the children, as the two girls had to share a bedroom and Martin was cramped in a small room, but Alan and I were delighted to be free of debt."55 Alan was pleased to discover that his close drinking companion, Alan Corker, lived next door.

As Alan's health improved, he declared he wished to spend some time in Cornwall. This was arranged by Rose Hilton, who introduced Alan and Valerie to Ben John, Augustus John's grandson, who was looking for someone he knew who could spend a few weeks in the Old Fish Store, his mother's flat in Mousehole. She had recently moved into a home, and Ben didn't want the place empty over the summer - extra income would also be very acceptable. The Lowndes fitted the bill: a deal was done enabling them to spend five weeks there in the school holidays. The flat was full of drawings by Gwen and Augustus John, as well as paintings by members of the Newlyn School. Alan pitched up his easel by a window, which gave panoramic views across Mount's Bay. "All this was very different from the commercial holiday let we were used to, it felt a privilege to be there."56 Alan started painting, tenuously at first, but he was soon working to his committed best.

THE OLD FISH STORE, MOUSEHOLE, CORNWALL

13 ST. GEORGE'S ROAD, UPPER CAM, GLOUCESTERSHIRE, THE LOWNDES'S LAST HOME

55 & 56 Valerie Lowndes

They enjoyed a very happy reunion with old friends, especially the Frosts, who had moved to Newlyn. Terry Frost's oldest son Adrian, the Monwets, Nathalie Featherstone (separated from Bill), Rose Hilton and others called in to congratulate Alan on his recovery.[57] In between visitors Alan usually worked, but he and Valerie walked round the harbour at midday and called in at the Ship for a soft drink for Alan and a hard one for Valerie. They had a wonderful holiday at the Old Fish Store culminating in a party for about 30 people with many of their old friends. Alan was trying hard.

Alan painted four works while they were there, three seascapes and one of cottages in Mousehole. Soon after their return from Cornwall, Brian Bull organised a one-man show for Alan at the Bristol Arts Centre. These four works were displayed there and two were sold. In many ways the paintings of his last period were the best he ever painted; they had a new harder edge and were very confident works. Family life had become so much better for all; the old Alan had come back, not least his sense of humour. Rosalind told a lovely tale of the doctor's visit, when he was recuperating in bed. The doctor noticed a bottle of barley wine by the bed.

"You know you mustn't drink, it will kill you."
"I haven't had a drink, doctor."
"Are you sure you have not had a drink?"
"No doctor."
"Quite sure?"
"Would you like a light?" Alan struck a light on the 'bottle', which was of course a gimmicky lighter.

Alan received a card from Lord Bath, then Lord Weymouth, inviting him and Valerie to a buffet lunch at Longleat House for Wessex painters and their families. Lord Bath gave a talk explaining he wanted to start a gallery in his private apartments at Longleat showing paintings of Wessex. To this end he was buying paintings and wanted one by Alan. He subsequently wrote to Alan suggesting they went to lunch and asked him to bring a selection of work with a Wessex subject matter, from which he would select one. In November 1977 the meeting took place, where Lord Bath bought one of Alan's more recent paintings, 'Cottage in Slimbridge'. Interestingly Lord Bath does not recall Lowndes having a pronounced stutter at the luncheon. Perhaps this was a consequence of his Lordship's easy-going nature and eccentricities, which would have appealed hugely to Lowndes. Later Lord Bath wrote asking for another meeting, because he wanted to exchange the picture, at which he took an earlier work, 'Beer and Skittles'. There was also talk of a one-man show at Longleat, but Lord Bath insisted that all the paintings had to be of Wessex. Ideas were discussed in February 1978. Alan became keen on the idea and started work on a series of local scenes. Sadly illness and death were to intervene, the one-man show never took place.

Also in 1978 Alan and Valerie met Trevor Nunn and his wife, Janet Suzman. Janet already owned one of Alan's paintings, but wanted to purchase another. Once the meeting was arranged, they went to see Janet in a play at the Royal Court in London, and then met her and Trevor Nunn at the Chelsea Arts Club. Following a very convivial dinner with much talk about Shakespeare and the theatre, they bought the painting, 'Manx Railway Loco', which Alan had completed after visiting the Naughtons in the Isle of Man. Janet bought another, 'The Match Factory'. These sales were very important with Andras Kalman's stipend no longer available. Alan wrote about the meeting to Elizabeth Boston on December 15th, 1977. "We recently went out with Janet Suzman and Trevor Nunn for a supper. Janet found me interesting and kept kissing me (which I rather liked) but I caught her looking oddly at me from time to time."[58]

He had plans to go to Ireland in 1978, where as a member of the Chelsea Arts Club, he could enjoy the club's reciprocal agreement with the Arts Club in Dublin. From Dublin he intended to make a trip to Belfast, a town he knew quite well to "do some work there." If he got back in one piece, he planned to have an exhibition with Kalman in London. He continued in his letter to Elizabeth Horsfield, "About the life and limb risk I am not too worried. At the last check up I had, the Hospital specialists told me that I'd not got very

---

57 Bill Featherstone is a relatively mysterious figure, a Canadian sculptor and later a painter. He lived in the Penwith area in the sixties and then returned to Canada

58 The family and some friends are convinced Alan hardly touched alcohol after his health scare. Conversely Brian Bull in print and Alan Corker on tape attest that he did indeed start drinking again. Alan Corker refused to buy him an alcoholic drink when they first went out together, so Alan bought it for himself, starting with shandy and ending with several glasses of Guinness. From then on he consumed alcoholic drinks in his company, as he did in Brian Bull's; one has to presume he did the same with his other drinking friends.

long left anyway. I don't really believe in the specialists as they gave me up for dead when I was first in hospital."⁵⁹ He also had plans to live in Cornwall again or in France, when the children were launched on their various careers.

'COTTAGE IN SLIMBRIDGE'. *18 x 16 inches, Oil on Canvas, 1977 (Lord Bath initially bought this painting, which he later exchanged for 'BEER AND SKITTLES')*

59 Letter written by Alan Lowndes to Elizabeth Boston (Horsfield) 15th December. 1977

All his plans were to come to naught. Very sadly a year was all the family had. Alan became very ill again in August, 1978 and was taken to hospital. Valerie tells the story:

"For some years we had been friendly with Frank and Elizabeth Gadsby. Frank ran the Pallas Gallery and had commissioned Alan to make several lithographs. We met them both in London and Gloucestershire and also in Marlborough, where they had a summerhouse. Their children were of a similar age to ours, and we had lunches with them there two or three times every summer. That fateful August, in 1978, we were there for Sunday lunch. During the afternoon, Alan started to complain of a pain in his upper arm. I didn't pay too much attention, though Frank was quite concerned.

After we returned home, the pain progressively worsened, but the doctor refused to come out for a triviality, as she saw it. After a very distressing week, the pain becoming excruciating, he fell into a deep sleep for which I was thankful, but when our friend Ann Harris, a nurse, called and saw his condition, she quickly rang the surgery and insisted that a doctor come straight away. Ann's intervention had the desired effect, and the doctor finally came. Alan was now diagnosed as diabetic, and was apparently almost sinking into a coma, so an emergency ambulance was called to rush him to hospital. I followed, and on examination at the hospital, it was discovered that Alan's pain was caused by a large abscess inside his arm, which had to be removed. The medication he subsequently received upset his damaged liver, as a result of which he became very ill, so different medication was given. After about two weeks, the doctor told me he had a 50/50 chance of recovery, and from then on he improved day by day. Jack Harris and I took it in turns to visit every evening, and were both very encouraged. We'd had to cancel our family holiday in St. Ives, booked for August, but now Alan was so much stronger we planned to go on our own, the children now back at school and old enough to look after themselves for a week or two. We both looked forward to this.

Sadly, Alan's health suddenly deteriorated, and one afternoon I had a call from the hospital: he had started to haemorrhage internally. When I arrived he was asleep, and looking very pale. The doctors were conferring on whether they could perform an operation to stop the bleeding, but eventually decided he was too weak, and there was nothing they could now do. Christopher Hull, from the Annexe Gallery in Wimbledon, was also at the hospital to visit Alan. He had given him a solo exhibition in 1978 and had become a friend, so we commiserated with each other. I said good night to Alan, who did stir and speak to me, then went home to tell the children he was dying."

Amanda Lowndes continues in her diary:

"Thursday 21st September, 1978

. . . Mum phoned from hospital to say she'd been there most of the day, and dad was worse - he's bleeding from inside or something, and they're giving him a transfusion, but he's too weak to operate on. Doesn't sound at all good - it's pretty bad, they say, so that depressed me. This was about 5.00 p.m. . . .

Monday 25th September, 1978

This weekend has just been so sad and so long - I'm not going to write much or I'll get upset again, and I've just begun to accept it. Dad died on Friday morning. That sounds so cold and horrible - it was just terrible. I hadn't realised he was that ill, or at least, I'd just assumed he'd pull through like he did last time - but when mum came into our bedroom on Friday morning, about 7.30, and said she'd phoned the hospital and they thought he was going. Rosalind and I just cried in each other's arms at the thought. Then mum, Martin and I went to the hospital. Rosalind couldn't face it and stayed at home with Sally and Gail. It was terrible - and yet in a way, I'm glad I went. The thought of him going without us there - without me even, was horrible - although he was unconscious and we couldn't speak to him. We just sat by the bed and watched him. They were pumping blood into him and he had an oxygen mask on. He was breathing deeply, and looked so pale and frail and delicate

- but blissfully peaceful and unaware, almost child-like and innocent, and he just stopped breathing gradually, it was very peaceful, thank god. But us three - Martin looked so terribly unhappy - oh hell, it was awful, we just cried and cried. At the time, I just wanted to speak to him and tell him we all love him and I didn't mean any of the nasty things I'd said to him over the years. But I suppose if we had spoken it would have been so heart-rending, and I wouldn't have been able to stop crying, I know. God, can't go on writing this. Over the weekend we saw lots of people who came to see us and say how sorry they were, the phone's been going all the time, we've had lots of letters . . ."

The funeral was set for Thursday, September 28th, 1978 in St. John's Church. Valerie wore Alan's velvet jacket. Many came to the funeral. Anne Willett said it was only the second time in her life she had seen her husband in tears. Alan Corker was so upset by Alan's death, he could not sleep at all before the funeral. Next day he found he just could not bring himself to attend the service and stood some hundred yards away. He became aware of another figure by him, who also could not make himself attend, a grey haired man with tears streaming down saying "How sad, how sad". Andras Kalman had made the funeral. Jack Harris and friends left the service singing Alan's favourite song 'Bye Bye Blackbird. If I were a blackbird, I would whistle and sing'.

Some time has passed since Alan's death, and it is easier to make a judgement about his paintings. Writers and artists today can make more objective comments on Alan's paintings without contemporary pressures. Nevertheless his family and friends must wince when they still read critics today adopting the intellectually lazy habit of using labels, such as 'naive painter' to describe his works. We can only assume they have never really looked at his paintings.

Jonathan Benington, gallery curator and author, wrote in 2008, "I much enjoyed seeing 3 works by Alan at the Stockport Art Gallery and felt that the town should do more to honour such a distinguished local painter, perhaps starting with a decent retrospective exhibition/catalogue … His work has grit and integrity, the smell and grease of the street, a refreshing absence of airs and graces, and that's why I like him. He was one of a dying breed, perhaps, in the sense that he remained true to his proletariat roots."

The potter and Turner Prize winner, Grayson Perry wrote to the author in 2008 explaining why he chose Lowndes's pictures for his superb exhibition 'Unpopular Culture', "I liked Alan's paintings, particularly 'Telling the Tale' because they demonstrate those timeless qualities that all good painters have, the ability to put colours together in an exciting yet harmonious way and an intuitive grasp of compositional drama. These are the essence of beautiful painting and cannot be faked. There is also a very English humility in the works, which I respond to warmly. He has a distinctive visual language that seems to have grown organically out of his love of painting, it is at once rich yet also restrained. I also like the telling details like the R.N.L.I. collecting box."

Alan was introduced by Brian Bull to a young painter from Bristol, Barrington Tabb. Barrington has become quite a celebrity in the Bristol area and a highly respected painter. He was very impressed by Alan's paintings, but also knew that Alan could be thunderous one minute and gentle the next depending on his alcohoilc state. He was especially concerned when Alan was telephoned by Andras Kalman, which always resulted in several quick drinks afterwards, before any paintings were shown. Barrington, known as Barry to the Lowndes family, regarded Alan as a great help to him as an artist. He was very impressed by his choice and use of colour, his feeling for paint and his observation of what happens in the community. He learned a great deal from Alan's ability to simplify the compostion. As Barrington said, "Alan was on his own. I of course knew Lowry's work, but Alan's sophisticated simplification, sense of design and the way he moved paint around put him at a higher level than Lowry."

Lowndes may have been erratic in his production and very difficult at times, but there is no doubt that he painted very few failures throughout his life. No one can be at his or her best all the time, however it is very rare to discover an artist whose standard remained so constant as Lowndes; apart from some of his early pastiches, it is very difficult to discover a poorly composed or executed picture. This is quite remarkable considering his health and alcohol related problems. History is judging him to be a major painter, even perhaps one day bearing out Terry Frost's and Barrington Tabb's favourable comparison between Lowndes and Lowry. Andras Kalman summed up Lowndes very well at the Stockport Retrospective in 1973, "You can't be clever. I see something original and very honest and unique. What makes a great painter? The answer must be he adds something original and personal to the history or repertoire of painting, and Alan Lowndes does that."

In conclusion, it is impossible to judge someone by a consistent or arbitrary standard. Behaviour and attitudes that are obnoxious in one person are tolerated in another. In this sense it is extremely difficult to describe in writing human actions without falling into this judgemental trap. Perhaps it would be best to leave the final comment to one of Alan's friends, Brian Bull. "With all his faults and they were many, we all loved Alan. I feel sure knowing him was a great experience that did in some ways change our outlook on life. Basically he was a very good and warm hearted man, who lived for his work and truly felt life had not rewarded him as it should."

Postscript from Valerie Lowndes:

"In the Spring of 1979 the children and I went to St. Ives for a holiday. Willie Barnes Graham had invited me into her lovely flat overlooking Porthmeor beach to give me her condolences and talk about art and life. Among many other things, she said, "It's a privilege to be married to an artist." I thought this a very curious thing to say, remembering the rows, the drinking and the constant money problems. But now, years later, my very selective memory has glossed over the many bad times, and I remember the talented, creative people I met, the friendships I have enjoyed and the small knowledge of art I have gained. I think she was right. It was a hard-earned thorny privilege."

The book has a fitting finale of some images of St. John's Church, the Churchyard, Alan's Gravestone and three of his pictures completed in his last year, 1978.

'In Loving Memory of Alan Lowndes Died 22nd September 1978 Aged 57 Years. May he Rest in Peace'

The Beautiful and Tranquil St. John's Churchyard, Upper Cam and Alan Lowndes's Gravestone somewhat obscured, foreground left.

'THE YEW TREE LEANING ON THE CHURCH' (ST. JOHN'S CHURCH, UPPER CAM), *30 x 20 inches, Oil on Board, February 1971 (Collection of David Messum Fine Art Limited)* The Lowndes family spent their first winter in Gloucestershire in 1971 and experienced colder weather than they had been used to in Cornwall, where snow was very rare.

RIGHT PAGE (233): 'LOVE AND THE BANDIT', *20 x 14 inches, Oil on Canvas, 1978 (Collection of the Artist)*

LEFT PAGE (234):
DETAIL OF 'OLD
GLOUCESTER BARGE',
23 x 20 inches, Oil on
Board, 1978 (Private
Collection)

'TARTED UP PUB', *16 x 22 inches, Oil on Canvas, 1978 (Collection of Stephen Gould)*

Drawings

Lowndes created hundreds of drawings, some quick sketches of figures and buildings to prepare for paintings and others more resolved and complete works in themselves; nearly all are interesting, capture the moment and are a tribute to his compositional skill. Unfortunately the dates of the drawings are unknown.

ABOVE LEFT: 'TWO WOMEN', *6.75 x 5 inches, Ink Wash*
ABOVE RIGHT: 'WOMAN, CHILD AND CAT, PLOVER COURT', *9.75 x 6 inches, Pencil*
LOWER LEFT: 'SHETLANDS', *9 x 10 inches, Ink Wash*
LOWER RIGHT: DETAIL OF 'TWO WOMEN RECUMBENT', *7.5 x 9.75 inches, Colour Wash and Pencil*

Top: 'Man and Horse', *10.5 x 8.5 inches*, Ink Wash
Below: 'Woman Lying on her Back', *13 x 19 inches*, Pastel and Pencil

'GIRL WITH HAT'. 19.5 x 13.5 *inches, Pencil*

Top: 'Boat', 4 x 6 inches, Colour wash
Below Left: Detail of 'Nude Leaning on Elbow', 7 x 10 inches, Pencil
Below Right: 'Three Circus Girls', 13 x 10 inches, Ink wash

'TEA TIME'. *19.5 x 13.5 inches, Crayon*

ABOVE: 'FACTORY CHIMNEY'. *14.5 x 9.5. Pencil*
BELOW: 'VILLAGE'. *9.5 x 13.75 inches, Crayon*

241

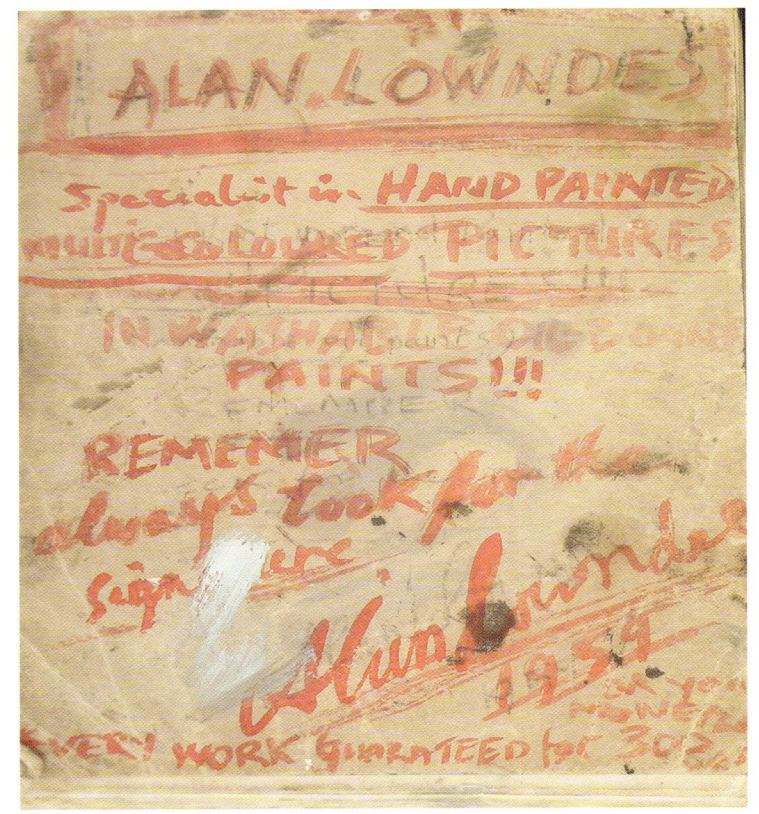

LEFT: *Cover of a sketch book dated 1959 with typical Lowndes humour scribbled all over it. He was living at the time at 2 Canterbury Road, Stockport. The book contains some 55 quick sketches of circus animals and performers completed when he was given permission to observe the Belle Vue Circus in Manchester. A selection from the sketchbook is illustrated below and page right.*

Size: 11 x 9 inches, Ink Wash and/or Pencil

243

Illustrated Paintings

As far as possible, titles are those given to the paintings by Alan Lowndes in the manner he wrote them on the painting itself or elsewhere. Cataloguing has been difficult; many titles were changed over the years. Almost all Lowndes's paintings were exhibited at the Crane Gallery in Manchester or at the Crane Kalman Gallery in London. Mention has been made of the Crane Gallery Exhibition in 1956, largely because Kalman considered it a very important exhibition, otherwise only Galleries other than Kalman's have been noted.

Page	Title
2 -	Detail from Two Musical Clowns
6 -	Self Portrait to Cilli
10 -	Lancashire Street
15 -	Chip Shop
16 -	Aunt Dora's Shop
17 -	The Barrow
18 -	Cart by William Turner
21 -	Italian Hill Village
22 -	Italian Village
23 -	Florence
24 -	Mrs. Clare's St. Bernard
24 -	Fountain, Florence
27 -	Demolishing Lancashire Hill - *Exhibited: Neptune Theatre 1968*
30 -	Tom Hassell
30 -	Dancing Girls
31 -	Stockport Market - *Exhibited: Stockport Museum and Art Gallery 1972; Annexe Gallery, Wimbledon 1977; Stockport Museum and Art Gallery 1979*
33 -	Street, Florence
33 -	War Damage Assisi
33 -	The Baker's Vaults
34 -	Girl Wading - *Exhibited: Stockport Museum and Art Gallery 1972; Stockport Museum and Art Gallery 1979; Singer Museum, Laren 1980*
34 -	Back Alley Girl - *Exhibited: Crane Gallery, Manchester 1956; Stockport Museum and Art Gallery 1972; Penwith Gallery 1979*
35 -	Man and Dog - *Exhibited: Stockport Museum and Art Gallery 1979 as 'Man and Whippet'*
36/37 -	Power and the Glory - *Exhibited: Crane Gallery, Manchester 1956*
38/39 -	Stockport Market Place
40 -	Reyberolle, Self portrait
41 -	The Organ Grinder - *Exhibited: Stockport Museum and Art Gallery 1972; Stockport Museum and Art Gallery 1979; Atkinson Gallery 1979; Singer Museum, Laren 1980*
42 -	The Pawn Shop - *Exhibited: The John Moores Liverpool Exhibition, 1959*
43 -	The Back Street
44 -	Let Go You Bully - *Exhibited: Stockport Museum and Art Gallery 1972*
45 -	Middle Hill Gate - *Exhibited: Prospect Gallery, London 1956, wrongly titled 'Middle Mill Gate'*
46 -	Pub Scene - *Exhibited: Stockport Museum and Art Gallery 1972; Stockport Museum and Art Gallery 1979; Singer Museum, Laren 1980*
46 -	Sylvan Grove - *Exhibited: Crane Gallery, Manchester 1956; Prospect Gallery, London 1956; Stockport Museum and Art Gallery 1972; Stockport Museum and Art Gallery 1979; Penwith Gallery 1979; Atkinson Gallery 1979*
47 -	The Arches, Stockport - *Exhibited: Crane Gallery, Manchester 1956; Prospect Gallery, London 1956*
47 -	Gasworks - *Exhibited: Prospect Gallery, London 1956; Stockport Museum and Art Gallery 1979*
48 -	Children in the Street - The exact title of this work is not known. The title given in the book was as written in a letter from the owner, Jim Lovelock, to Andras Kalman
49 -	Lunatic Cat
50 -	In the Park - *Exhibited: Stockport Museum and Art Gallery 1972; Stockport Museum and Art Gallery 1979*
51 -	Portrait of Cilli
53 -	Pot Shrigley Farm
54 -	Alley Cat - *Exhibited: Prospect Gallery, London 1956; 'Alley Cat' was featured on*

PAGE	TITLE
	B.B.C. Television's Twentieth Century Antiques Road Show in 2005
57 -	Crane Gallery, Manchester - *Exhibited: Stockport Museum and Gallery 1979*
58 -	Guinness Girl - *Exhibited: Crane Gallery, Manchester 1956; Stockport Museum and Art Gallery 1972; Stockport Museum and Art Gallery 1979*
58 -	Mum Sweeping - *Exhibited: Stockport Museum and Art Gallery, 1972 (The painting was incorrectly dated as 1963 in the catalogue); Neptune Theatre, Liverpool 1968; Stockport Museum and Art Gallery 1979; Singer Museum, Laren 1980*
58 -	Street Market (Possibly Market Place) - *Exhibited: Stockport Museum and Art Gallery 1972; Stockport Museum and Art Gallery 1979*
59 -	Girl Standing
59 -	Walking Day - *Exhibited: Stockport Museum and Art Gallery 1979*
60 -	Lancashire Hill
60 -	Stockport Street Scene: *Possibly exhibited at Bradford City Art Gallery 1961*
61 -	Stockport Mill
62 -	Wash Night (Also titled 'Bath Night' and 'Friday Night') - *Exhibited: Crane Gallery, Manchester 1956; Stockport Museum and Art Gallery 1972*
62 -	Seated Nude - *Exhibited: Stockport Museum and Art Gallery 1972; Stockport Museum and Art Gallery 1979; Singer Museum, Laren 1980*
63 -	Two Women Walking
66 -	Flowers in a Jar - *Exhibited: Stockport Museum and Art Gallery 1972; Stoke on Trent Museum and Art Gallery 1986*
68 -	The Actor (Charles Laughton)
68 -	A Cup of Tea. Elsa Lanchester and Joyce Redmond
69 -	The D'Jango Club, Manchester
70 -	The Kiss
72/73 -	Coronation Street
80 -	Eagles Nest, Where no Vultures Fly
81 -	Street Corner - *Exhibited: Crane Gallery, Manchester 1956*
82 -	The Quay - *Exhibited: Stockport Museum and Art Gallery 1979*
83 -	The Harbour
84/85 -	The Accordion Player - *Exhibited: Annexe Gallery, Wimbledon 1977; Royal West of England Academy 1980, City Museum and Art Gallery, Worcester 1985*
86 -	Fishing Boat off Smeaton's Pier
87 -	Logan Rock, Rosewall Hill - *Exhibited: Royal West of England Academy 1980*
88 -	Man in Boat
90 -	Self Portrait - *Exhibited: Osborne Gallery, New York 1964; Annexe Gallery, Wimbledon 1977*
91 -	Portrait of Janet, Stockport (Also titled 'Girl in Green') - *Exhibited: Crane Gallery, Manchester 1956*
92 -	Carole
93 -	Janet Recumbent, Stockport
94 -	Fairground Girl
95 -	Clowns Boxing Match - *Exhibited: Stockport Museum and Art Gallery 1979*
96 -	Three Musical Clowns - *Exhibited: John Moores Exhibition, Liverpool 1961; Royal West of England Academy 1980*
97 -	Three Practicing Equilibrists
103 -	Washing Day - *Exhibited: Stockport Museum and Art Gallery 1979*
104 -	Ice Cream Man - *Exhibited: Prospect Gallery, London 1956; Exhibited as 'Ice Cream Seller', Stockport Museum and Art Gallery 1972*
105 -	Dancing Girls
106 -	Rosemary Street, Stockport
107 -	Cat Bewildered
108 -	High Street, Stockport
112 -	To Valerie with Love - *Exhibited: Royal West of England Academy 1980*
113 -	The Studio, Vence
118 -	Tourette sur Loupe - *Exhibited: Royal West of England Academy 1980*
119 -	Portrait of John Milne: *Exhibited: Penwith Gallery 1979*
121 -	Portrait of Sydney Graham - *Exhibited: Penwith Gallery 1979; Royal West of England Academy 1980*
124 -	March Fair
125 -	Boy and his Donkey - *Exhibited: Prospect Gallery, London 1956 (Titled: Boy with Pony); Stockport Museum and Art Gallery 1972 (Titled: The Boy with Pony);*

PAGE	TITLE
	Stockport Museum and Art Gallery 1979 (Titled Boy and his Pony); Penwith Gallery 1979; Singer Museum, Laren 1980
126 -	Mealhouse Brow - *Exhibited: Stockport Museum and Art Gallery 1972*
128 -	Ship off St. Ives
128 -	Yellow Bathing Suit
129 -	The Gamblers - *Exhibited: Osborne Gallery, New York 1964; Neptune Theatre, Liverpool 1968*
130 -	Plover Court
131 -	Mandy and Martin
132 -	Ros on Pony
132 -	Mandy on Tonto
132 -	Ros by Flowers
133 -	Rosewall Hill - *Exhibited: Stockport Museum and Art Gallery 1972*
134/135	Beach Scene (1964) - *Exhibited: Atkinson Art Gallery 1965; The New Ashgate Gallery 1976; The Annexe Gallery, Wimbledon 1977; The Royal West of England Academy 1980; City Museum and Art Gallery, Worcester 1985; The Tate Gallery, 'St. Ives 1995 - A Century of Images' (Titled: Porthmeor Beach)*
138 -	Telling the Tale - *Exhibited: Osborne Gallery, New York 1964; Unpopular Culture 2008-2009*
139 -	Entering the Circus - *Exhibited: Osborne Gallery, New York 1964; Unpopular Culture 2008-2009*
142 -	Beach Scene (1963)
143 -	The Old Organ Grinder - *Exhibited: Stockport Museum and Art Gallery 1972; The Atkinson Gallery 1979*
143 -	Nude and Fig Tree - *Exhibited: Annexe Gallery, Wimbledon 1977; Royal West of England Academy 1980*
144 -	Stormy Sunset
144 -	Watery Sunset - *Exhibited: The Tate Gallery, 'St. Ives 1997 - Mixed Exhibition'*
145 -	Serene Sunset
146 -	A Village School
146 -	Shooting Range
147 -	The Big Chimney - *Exhibited: Stockport Museum and Art Gallery 1972*
147 -	Three Boats
148 -	Two Old Cronies
152/153	The Land's End - *Exhibited: Stockport Museum and Art Gallery 1972*
154 -	Painter and Critics - *Exhibited: Osborne Gallery, New York 1964; Neptune Theatre, Liverpool 1968; Penwith Gallery 1979; Royal West of England Academy 1980; Tate Gallery, St. Ives 'Artists on Artists', chosen by Terry Frost 2003*
155 -	Terry Frost: Red Circle Black
156 -	Simeon Stafford: Fish and Chips
160 -	Paddys Brow - *Exhibited: Neptune Theatre, Liverpool 1968*
161 -	The Ancient Mariner
161 -	The Snack Waggon
162 -	AR Mill - *Exhibited: Neptune Theatre, Liverpool 1968*
163 -	Chestergate
164 -	The Portwood Bridge
166/167	Setting up Stalls - *Exhibited: Stockport Museum and Art Gallery 1972*
168 -	Rosewall Hill, Winter
169 -	Man, Cat and Boat - *Exhibited: Stockport Museum and Art Gallery 1979; Penwith Gallery 1979; Singer Museum, Laren 1980*
170/171	Champ and Challenger
172 -	The Goal Kick
173 -	St. Ives Harbour
174 -	The Surprise Attack
175 -	PZ 63
176 -	Going Home Christmas Eve
180 -	Railway Inn - *Exhibited: Royal West of England Academy 1980*
181 -	Darts Practice
182 -	Top Lane
183 -	Flower in Bottle
184 -	A Drunk Man
185 -	Love Lane Corner - *Exhibited: Stockport Museum and Art Gallery 1972; Stockport*

PAGE	TITLE
	Museum and Art Gallery 1979; Singer Museum, Laren 1980
186 -	Old Dosshouse - *Exhibited: Stockport Museum and Art Gallery 1972; Stockport Museum and Art Gallery 1979*
192 -	Stockport - Lithographic print
193 -	The Pawn Shop - Lithographic print
195 -	Ships Stores Merchant, Tiger Bay, Cardiff - *Exhibited: Stockport Museum and Art Gallery 1979*
196 -	Louisa Street, Tiger Bay, Cardiff
197 -	Eleanor Street, Tiger Bay, Cardiff
198/199	Stuart Street, Tiger Bay, Cardiff
201 -	Cardiff Street Scene
202 -	The Strong Man - *Exhibited Stockport Museum and Art Gallery 1979; Penwith Gallery 1980; Singer Museum, Laren 1980*
203 -	The Football Match - *Cover of 'Football Report, an Anthology of Soccer'*
206 -	A Memorial Tree
209 -	Girl Undressing
211 -	Pont Neuf, Dieppe
212 -	The Market House
213 -	Chatting on the Doorstep
214 -	The Rectory Farm, Slimbridge
215 -	The Darts Players
216 -	At Band Practice - *Exhibited: Penwith Gallery, 1979; Royal West of England Academy, 1980*
217 -	Two Friends Meeting
218 -	A Clean Sweep
219 -	Brace Girdles Count
220 -	Hill in Snow - *Exhibited: Singer Museum, Laren 1980*
222 -	No Through Road - *Exhibited: Atkinson Gallery 1979*
224 -	The Yellow Chair
227 -	Cottage in Slimbridge - *Exhibited: Stockport Museum and Art Gallery 1979; Penwith Gallery 1979; Royal West of England Academy 1980*
232 -	The Yew Tree Leaning on the Church
233 -	Love and the Bandit - *Exhibited: Stockport Museum and Art Gallery 1979; Penwith Gallery 1979; Royal West of England Academy 1980; City Museum and Art Gallery, Worcester 1985*
234 -	Old Gloucester Barge - *Exhibited: Stockport Museum and Art Gallery 1979; Penwith Gallery 1979; Royal West of England Academy 1980*
235 -	Tarted up Pub - *Exhibited: Stockport Museum and Art Gallery 1979; Penwith Gallery 1979; Royal West of England Academy 1980*

Drawings

236 -	Two Women
	Woman, Child and Cat, Plover Court
	Shetlands
	Two Women Recumbent
237 -	Man and Horse
	Woman Lying on her Back
238 -	Woman with Hat
239 -	Boat
	Nude Leaning on her Elbow
	Three Circus Girls
240 -	Tea Time
241 -	Factory Chimney
	Village
242-243	Cover and a selection from Sketch Book, 1959

Postscript: The author would be delighted to receive further information about the illustrated paintings or about any other pictures people may own. Records have been sparse, any extra assistance would be much appreciated, especially for completing the Catalogue Raisonné.

Exhibition List

One-man Exhibitions

1951 The Stockport Arms, 25 St. Petersgate, Stockport, March
1952 Crane Gallery Manchester, 'Alan Lowndes, Thirty Six Paintings', March
1953 County Hotel, Stockport
1955 Crane Gallery, Manchester, February
1956 Crane Gallery Manchester, 'Paintings by Alan Lowndes', Feb. 14 - Mar. 9
1956 Prospect Gallery, 13 Duke Street, St. James, London, 'Paintings 1949 to 1956'
1957 Crane Kalman Gallery, London, 178 Brompton Road, London SW3, 'Alan Lowndes of Stockport', Oct. 17 - Nov. 2
1961 Crane Kalman Gallery, London, 'Alan Lowndes', Dec. 14, 1961 - Jan. 13, 1962
1964 Osborne Gallery, New York, 'Alan Lowndes', April 14 - May 3
1965 Crane Kalman Gallery, London, 'Alan Lowndes', Dec. 10, 1965 - Jan. 16, 1966
1966 Crane Gallery, 35 South King Street, Manchester, 'Alan Lowndes of Stockport', June 8 - June 25
1967 Magdalene Street Gallery, Cambridge
1968 Crane Kalman Gallery, London, 'Alan Lowndes', April 25 - May 18
1968 Neptune Theatre, Liverpool, September
1968 Curlew Gallery, Lord Street, Southport, Dec. 7, 1968 - Jan. 11, 1969
1972 Crane Kalman Gallery, London, 'Recent Paintings by Alan Lowndes', April 20 - May 20
1972 Stockport Art Gallery, Greek Street, Stockport, 'Retrospective Exhibition', Sept. 23 - Oct. 14
1972 Rutland Gallery, 29 Bruton Street, London, Nov. 28 - Dec. 30
1973 Turnpike Gallery, Leigh, Lancashire, 'Retrospective Exhibition of Paintings 1948-72', Jan. 9 - Jan. 27
1976 Crane Kalman Gallery, London, 'Alan Lowndes, a Selection of Paintings', Feb. 24 - Mar. 20
1977 Annexe Gallery, 45 Wimbledon High Street, London, 'Alan Lowndes - A Selection of Paintings', April 30 - May 28, 1977
1977 Arts Centre, Bristol, 'Paintings of Alan Lowndes', September
1978 Crane Kalman Gallery, London, 'Alan Lowndes : a selection of Paintings', Feb. 7 - Mar. 4
1979 Stockport Art Gallery, 'Alan Lowndes', June 9 - July 7
1979 Penwith Galleries, 'Alan Lowndes 1948 to 1978', Aug. 18 - Sept. 6
1979 Atkinson Gallery, Southport, Dec. 1 - Dec. 22
1980 Royal West of England Academy, Bristol, Sept. 2 - 20
1980 Singer Museum, Oude Drift 1, Laren, Netherlands, 'Alan Lowndes 1921-1978', Dec. 13, 1980 - Jan. 18, 1981
1984 Crane Kalman Gallery, London, 'Alan Lowndes - Retrospective', May 9 - June 23
1991 Crane Kalman Gallery, London, 'Alan Lowndes - A Selection of Thirty Paintings', March 12 - April 13
1994 Sims Gallery, 22 Fore Street, St. Ives, 'Alan Lowndes', Jan. 29 - Feb. 12
1994 Emscote Lawn, Warwick, 'Alan Lowndes', September
1995 Crane Kalman Gallery, 'Alan Lowndes (1921-1978), Retrospective Exhibition', Oct. 24 - Dec. 2
2010 Stockport Museum and Art Gallery, Retrospective Exhibition and Book launch of 'Alan Lowndes' by Jonathan Riley, Friday February 19th; Exhibition: Saturday, February 20 - Monday, May 31
2010 Crane Kalman Gallery, 'Alan Lowndes - A Retrospective Exhibition', June 22 - July 31

Mixed Exhibitions

1950 Crane Gallery, Manchester. 'Craxton, Freud, Milner, Gilbert and Lowndes'. April
1950 Crane Gallery, Manchester.'Two Young Painters, Alan Lowndes and Richard Bridge'. September
1955 Lancashire Society of Artists
1959 Crane Kalman Gallery. 'Humour in Art'
1959 Walker Art Gallery Liverpool. 'John Moores Exhibition'
1960? (The date is not known) Sail Loft Gallery, St. Ives. 'Lowndes, Le Grice and Bill Featherstone'. July 9 - Aug. 4
1959 Crane Kalman Gallery, London. 'The Innocent Eye' Dec. 11, 1959 - Jan. 16, 1960
1960 Arts Council Tour. 'Northen Artists - Manchester, Sheffield, Newcastle-upon-Tyne, Bolton, Bradford, Carlisle'. July - December
1960 Crane Kalman Gallery, London. 'Mood of the North'. Nov. 9 - Dec. 3.
1961 Bradford City Art Gallery. 'Spring Exhibition'. March 29 - May 28
1962 Kuntsverein, Hanover. Malerie der Gegenwart aus Sudwestengland
1962 Crane Kalman Gallery. 'Painted in England, Four Uniquely English Artists': Sept. 20 - Oct. 20
1963 Sail Loft Gallery, St. Ives. Summer
1963 Walker Art Gallery, Liverpool. 'John Moores Exhibition'. Nov. 1963 - Jan. 1964
1963 Crane Kalman Gallery. 'The Englishness of English Painting'. Dec. 4, 1963 - Jan. 15, 1964
1963 Andrew Dickinson White Museum, Cornell University, New York. 'The Englishness of English Painting'. 1963 - 1964
1965 Walker Art Gallery, Liverpool. 'Industry and the Artist'. Feb. 28 - March 28
1965 Crane Kalman Gallery. '4 Literary Painters'. March 18 - April 15
1965 Atkinson Gallery, Southport. Mixed Exhibition. May 29 - Aug. 29
1967 Crane Kalman Gallery. 'Modern British Painting'
1968 The Arts Council. 'Painting 1964 to 1967'
1968 Crane Kalman Gallery. 'Modern British Painting'
1969 Oestende Museum, Ostend - date not known, possibly 1969
1970 Crane Kalman Gallery. 'Modern British Painting'. Dec. 1, 1970 - Jan. 16, 1971
1976 New Ashgate Gallery, Farnham. First Exhibition : 'Sheila Fell, Alan Lowndes, L.S. Lowry and a group of Northern Primitive Painters, also sculpture by Ben Franklin'. April 6 - 29.
1979 Crane Kalman Gallery. 'L.S. Lowry 1887 - 1976 and Alan Lowndes 1921 - 1978 - A Comparison'. March 15 - April 4
1979 Atkinson Art Gallery, Southport. 'Town and Country : an Exhibition of Works by Alan Lowndes and Mary Newcomb'. Dec. 1 - 22
1983 Christopher Hull Gallery: 'Barrington Moore Tabb : with small exhibition of works by Alan Lowndes, 1923-1979'. July 6 - Aug. 6
1983 Arts Council. 'Landscape in Britain 1850 - 1950'
Hayward Gallery February 10th - April 17th
Bristol April 30th - June 4th
Stoke on Trent June 11th - July 16th
Sheffield July 23rd - August 28th
1985 Crane Kalman Gallery. 'Five very English Artists'. May 15 - June 15
1985 City Museum and Art Gallery Worcester. 'Cornish & Contemporary: a selection by Peter Davies of recent painting and sculpture in Cornwall: Robert Adams, Noel Betowski, Mary Fedden, John Gibbons, David Haughton, Alan Lowndes, Alastair Michie, Charlotte Moore, Tony O'Malley, Bryan Wynter'. Nov. 9 - Dec. 7
1986 Stoke-on-Trent City Art Gallery. 'The Flower Show'. July 26 - Sept. 7
1989 Pelter Sands Gallery, Bristol. 'A Northern School' - November
2001 Crane Kalman Gallery - Painted in England, Four Uniquely English Artists
2001 Crane Kalman Gallery - British, European and American Art
2002 Crane Kalman Gallery - British and American Art

(Lowndes has been included in mixed exhibitions evey year after 2002 at the Crane Kalman Gallery)

Mixed Exhibitions cont.

2002 John Martin, London: 'Twentieth Century Painting & Sculpture : L.S. Lowry, Henry Moore, Laura Knight, Alberto Morrocco, Beatrice How, Sheila Fell, Alan Lowndes, John Piper, Mary Fedden, Josef Herman, Vincent Bennett, John Bratby, Elisabeth Frink, Jack Knox, Anthony Eyton, Derek Hill, Gwen John, William Crosbie', April 6 - 29.

2008/2009/2010 'Unpopular Culture': Grayson Perry selects from the Arts Council Collection May 10 - July 6, 2008 De la Warr Pavilion, Bexhill on Sea
July 19 - September 14, 2008 Harris Museum, Preston
September 27 - November 8, 2008 Royal Museum and Art Gallery, Canterbury
November 29, 2008 - January 4, 2009 DLI Museum and Durham Art Gallery, Durham
January 16 - March 15, 2009 Southampton City Art Gallery, Southampton
March 21 - May 10, 2009 Aberystwyth Arts Centre, Aberystwyth
May 16 - July 5, 2009 Scarborough Art Gallery, Scarborough
July 18 - October 25, 2009 Longside Gallery, Wakefield
November 7, 2009 - January 3, 2010 Victoria Art Gallery, Bath

Works held by the Tate Gallery

Dartsman and Organ Grinder 1972
Lithograph on paper, image: 505 x 657 mm
Presented by Curwen Studio through the Institute of Contemporary Prints 1975
The work exists in an Edition of 100 + 10 Artist's Proofs and it was published by Crane Kalman Gallery.

The Doss House 1975
Lithograph on paper, image: 511 x 410 mm
Presented by Curwen Studio through the Institute of Contemporary Prints 1975
The artist has also confirmed this information plus the fact that the work exists in an Edition of 100 + 7 Artist's Proofs. It was published by Pallas Gallery.

The Pawnbroker 1975
Lithograph on paper, image: 495 x 413 mm
Presented by Curwen Studio through the Institute of Contemporary Prints 1975
The artist has also confirmed this information plus the fact that the work exists in an Edition of 100 + 10 Artist's Proofs. It was published by Pallas Gallery.

Stockport Viaduct 1973
Lithograph on paper, image: 410 x 502
Presented by Curwen Studio

Index

Abse, Dannie - 200
Bacon, Francis - 120, 121
Baker's Vaults Pub - 32, 33, 40
Ballard, Arthur - 66, 67
Bamford House, Stockport (Lowndes's studio) - 30, 98, 99
Barnes-Graham, Wilhelmina - 120, 165, 230
Barstow, Stan - 41
Bath, Lord - 226, 227
Belle Vue Circus - 94, 242
Benington, Jonathan - 229
Benjamin, Anthony - 120
Berger, John - 40, 101, 111
Berlin, Helga - 77
Berlin, Sven - 77, 179
Bernstein, Lord Sidney - 67, 70
Blank, Sir Victor - 89
Bloomfield House - 177, 194
Bolton, Martin - 155
Booth, J. - 30
Boston, Ray - 52, 67, 70, 76,
Boulting Brothers - 67
Bourne, Bob - 158
Bowen, Denis - 141
Bradley, Helen - 24
Bradshaw, John (Judge) - 35
Braine, John - 41
Braque, Georges - 56
Bratby, John - 40
Brecht, Bertolt - 109
Breughel, Pieter - 102
Buffet, Bernard - 41
Bull, Brian - 177, 179, 180, 205, 222, 226, 229, 230
Caddick, Arthur - 179
Canney, Michael - 123
Cardiff - 151, 165, 177, 194-201
Carey, Joyce - 40
Chagall, Marc - 32
Chamberlain, Neville - 19
Chelsea Arts Club - 141, 226
Christchurch C.E. School - 11, 12
Churchill, Winston - 21
Clark, Bill - 63, 108, 129, 168, 175, 182, 220
Clayton, William - 30
Clowes, Frieda - 29, 51, 56, 75, 81
Conn, Roy - 120
Constable, John - 34
Contemporary Art Society of Wales - 194, 200, 201
Corker, Alan - 123, 177, 179, 225, 226, 229
Coronation Street - 1, 70, 71, 191
County Hotel, Stockport - 49, 52, 98, 99, 100, 188
Coutts-Smith, Kenneth - 141
Crabtree, Thomas - 77
Crane Gallery, Manchester - 29, 41, 55, 57, 64, 65, 67, 71, 75, 77, 80, 111
Craxton, John - 56, 67
Crossley, Bob - 120, 157
Curwen Press - 191, 192, 193, 194
Davies, Peter - 207
da Vinci, Leonardo - 150
De Bosmelet, Baroness Diana - 116, 117
De Chirico, Giorgio - 32
Delaney, Arthur - 102
Demount, Marion - 8, 25, 27
Dieppe - 109, 110, 111, 114, 115, 116, 211

Digey, The - 77, 119, 120, 132, 150
Dolan, Pat - 149, 177, 194, 222
Dooley, Arthur - 67, 159
Downside House - 189, 190
Doyle, Zena - 52
Drayson, Arthur - 98
Elfrick, Reverend Peter - 27
Emmanuel, John and Judi - 149
Epstein, Jacob - 56
Fallon, Conor - 123, 158,
Fauves - 32
Featherstone, Bill, Natalie - 158, 165, 226
Finney, Albert - 74
Florence - 21, 23, 24, 25, 32, 33, 93
Fontaine, Dick - 98
Fra Angelico - 21
Frank, Julius - 28, 29, 30, 32, 34, 40, 44
Freud, Lucian - 55, 56, 57, 67
Frost, Anthony - 151, 154, 155, 156
Frost, Sir Terry - 7, 119, 120, 121, 150, 151, 154, 155, 205, 207, 210, 226, 230
Frost, Wally - 179
Gadsby, Frank and Elizabeth - 228
Gale, Ian - 41, 101
Gardeners' Question Time - 52
Georges - 112, 114, 115, 116
Gibbs, Dr. - 194
Gimpel Fils Gallery - 56
Giotto - 21
Goaldiggers Trust - 204
Goldfield, Betty - 68, 69, 105
Goodman, Bill - 98
Gosling, Arthur - 5, 94
Gould, Stephen - 211, 215, 235
Gozzoli, Benozzo - 21
Graham, Sydney - 88, 119, 121, 122, 123, 149, 158, 177, 187, 189, 190, 205, 222, 223
Grimond, Jo - 74
Halestown - 119, 132, 142, 149, 157, 159, 177
Hall, Willis - 70, 204
Harper, Reverend John - 149
Harris, Jack - 179, 205, 228, 229
Harty, Russell - 70
Hassell, Antonia - 30, 120, 150
Hassell, Tom - 25, 29, 30, 102, 150
Heard, Michael - 121
Henri, Adrian - 159
Hepworth, Barbara - 79, 119, 123, 141
Heron, Patrick - 79, 80, 120, 121, 205
Hilton, Roger - 123, 205, 207, 225
Hilton, Rose - 225, 226
Hitler, Adolf - 19, 28, 116
Hoggart, Richard - 51
Hollard, Michel - 116, 117
Hollis and Vine - 25
Hopper, Edward - 41
Horrocks, Lieutenant General Sir Brian - 117
Horsfield, Dr. John - 52
Horsfield, Elizabeth (Cilli) - 7, 12, 29, 51, 52, 54, 67, 70, 75, 76, 79, 118, 191, 226, 227, 228
Horsfield, Nicholas - 60, 65, 66, 102, 111, 178, 206
Hotel D'Iena, Paris - 114
Hull, Christopher - 228
Hunt, Michael - 123
Huntington-Whitely, James - 203

Huxley, Aldous - 205
Ibiza and Formeterra - 114
Igel, Manya - 148
Ingram, Slim - 8, 11, 14, 17, 21, 75, 102, 157, 159, 205
Jennifer - 79
Jimson, Gully - 40, 51
John, Augustus - 56
John, Ben - 225
Kalman, Andras - 5, 29, 32, 40, 51, 52, 55, 64, 65, 67, 70, 71, 76, 77, 78, 79, 89, 100, 101, 102, 109, 110, 111, 113, 114, 115, 118, 120, 126, 132, 141, 157, 158, 165, 183, 184, 185, 188, 191, 194, 204, 205, 206, 207, 222, 226, 229, 230
Karolyi Foundation, Vence - 111
Karolyi, Countess - 111, 112, 113, 114
Keats, John - 187
Kelly, Sir Gerald - 56
Kennedy, Stetson - 112, 114, 116
King's Cinema, Stockport - 26
Kirchner, Ernst Ludwig - 56
Kitchen Sink School - 40
Klimt, Gustav - 70
Lancashire Hill, Stockport - 26, 27, 60
Lanchester, Elsa - 67, 68, 70,
Lanyon, Peter - 120, 121, 123, 165
Larkin, Meriel (Goaldiggers Trust) - 204
Lassaly, Walter - 71
Laughton, Charles - 7, 67, 68, 69, 70, 157
Lawley, Sue - 154
Lawrence, David Herbert - 56
Le Grice, Jeremy - 123
Levy, Emmanuel - 28,
Liar, Billy - 41
Lobaire, Andre - 65, 66
Lovelock, Jim and Diane - 47, 49, 99, 100
Lowndes, Christine - 7, 19, 27
Lowndes, Colin - 7, 9, 12, 14, 19, 75, 110
Lowndes, Jenny - 7, 8, 9, 27, 28
Lowndes, Jenny (née Murray) - 7, 8
Lowndes, John - 14
Lowndes, Mae - 11, 14, 157
Lowndes, Mandy - 8, 120, 131, 132, 146, 150, 158, 159, 178, 189, 191, 228
Lowndes, Martin - 120, 131, 158, 177, 178, 190, 191, 222, 225, 228, 229
Lowndes, Peter - 9
Lowndes, Rosalind - 120, 131, 132, 158, 177, 189, 191, 205, 226, 228
Lowndes, Sam (Father) - 7, 8, 9, 11, 12, 18, 75, 111, 158
Lowndes, Sam (Grandfather) - 9
Lowndes, Sam (Junior) - 7, 8, 9, 11, 14, 19, 66, 75, 102, 110, 157
Lowndes, Stanley - 7
Lowry, Laurence Stephen - 7, 21, 41, 55, 89, 101, 102, 113, 123, 126, 150, 154, 229, 230
Lucas, Andrew - 40
Lucas, Cornel - 41, 142
Machin, Frank - 25
Macintosh, Michael - 24
Major, Theodore - 102
Matisse, Henri - 30, 32, 44, 102
McGough, Roger - 159
McNay, Michael - 74, 102
Medwin, Michael - 179

Michelangelo - 21
Middleditch, Edward - 40
Milne, John - 119, 120
Mitchell, Denis - 120, 121, 123, 165, 226
Mitchell, Jane - 123
Monet, Claude - 110
Moore, Henry - 65
Mullaly, Terrance - 102, 188
Naughton, Bill - 159, 178, 179, 222, 226
Neptune Theatre, Liverpool - 159, 160
New Vision Gallery - 141
New York - 28, 129, 136, 137, 138, 139, 140, 154
Newhaven - 110
Nicholson, Ben - 77, 79, 141
Nunn, Trevor - 226
O'Casey, Breon - 142
O'Malley, Tony - 120, 122, 158, 165, 222
Old Fish Store, Mousehole - 225
Osborne Gallery, New York - 129, 136, 137, 138, 139, 140, 210
Osborne, John - 41, 70
Palace Repertory Theatre, Sale - 75
Parkinson, Sir Michael - 5, 67, 94, 101, 169, 172, 204
Pelter Sands Gallery - 207, 208
Penwith Art Society/Gallery - 79, 123, 142, 149
Perry, Grayson - 137, 229
Picasso, Pablo - 30, 56, 88
Pope, Alex - 149
Popski (Lt. Col. Vladamir Peniakoff) - 56
Pott Shrigley, Shropshire - 53
Priestley, J.B. - 188
Produce Hall, Stockport Market Place - 40
Pugh, Aled - 177, 179
Pugh, Erica - 56
Railway, The - 179, 180
Rebeyrolle, Paul - 40
Redgrave, Bill - 77, 120
Redgrave, Mary (Boots) - 77, 120, 123, 149, 158, 165
Redgrave, Sir Michael - 67
Richardson, Tony - 71
Roedewald, Cosmo - 119
Rossetti, Dante Gabriel - 55
Royal Salford School of Art - 29
Ryder, Dr. T.A. - 178
Saatchi, Charles - 56
Scopes, Maureen - 94
Slimbridge Wildfowl Trust - 177, 226, 227
Sloop Inn - 119, 120, 121, 158, 159,
Smith, Jack - 40
Spanish Club, Manchester - 29
Spencer, Stanley - 11
St. George's Road, No. 13 - 225
St. Ives - 66, 75, 76, 77, 78, 79, 88, 89, 110, 113, 117, 119, 120, 122, 123, 128, 132, 133, 136, 141, 144, 149, 150, 154, 157, 165, 173, 175, 177, 188, 200, 210, 228, 230
St. John's Church, Upper Cam - 177, 178, 229, 230, 231, 232
St. Mary's Church, Stockport - 34, 35, 40
Stafford, Simeon - 156
Stockport College of Science and Technology - 17
Suddaby, Leon - 207
Sutton, Keith - 126

252

Suzman, Janet - 226
Swann, Michael and Elizabeth - 149
Sylvia - 77, 78
Tabb, Barrington - 229
Taylor, Peter - 116
Thomas, Ron - 19, 28, 29, 30, 32, 35, 40, 44,
    59, 60, 64, 65, 70, 75, 88, 98, 102, 111, 112
Tieuli, Givoanni - 150
Tinners Arms, Zennor - 127
Tomlinson, David - 74, 185
Topham, Nurse - 132
Tucker, Alan - 66
Turner, William - 18, 102,
Upper Cam - 123, 151, 177, 179, 189, 190, 206,
    225, 231
Van Gogh, Vincent - 80, 187
Venice - 21, 25, 40
Wainwright, John - 35
Walker, Jane Elizabeth - 24
Wall, Brian - 121, 165
Wallis, Alfred - 156, 179
Wang, Cilli - 52
Warren, Tony - 70
Waterhouse, Keith - 41, 70, 89
Welland, Colin - 70, 71
Weschke, Karl - 120, 121, 123, 205
White Lion Hotel, Stockport - 30
Wife Sale, Stockport Market - 30
Willett, Anne - 109, 110, 114, 115, 229
Willett, John - 32, 40, 55, 56, 57, 65, 66, 70, 71,
    80, 109, 110, 111, 114, 115, 116, 118, 176, 229
Wood, Alan - 177
Wood, Christopher - 156
Wynne-Jones, Nancy - 120, 121, 122, 123, 141,
    149, 158
Wynter, Bryan - 119, 120, 123, 158, 165, 207
Wynter, Monica - 119
Zennor - 79, 123, 127, 149